# HARE
# EASY THICK LINE
# COLOING BOOK

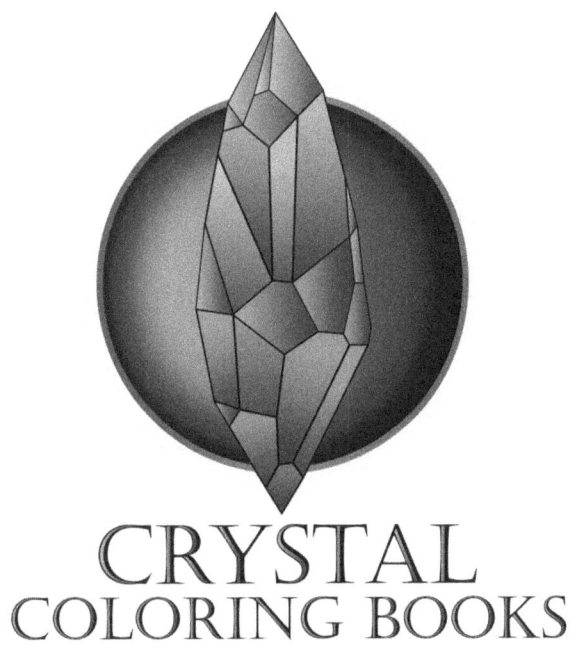

## CRYSTAL
### COLORING BOOKS

ISBN: 9781703049725

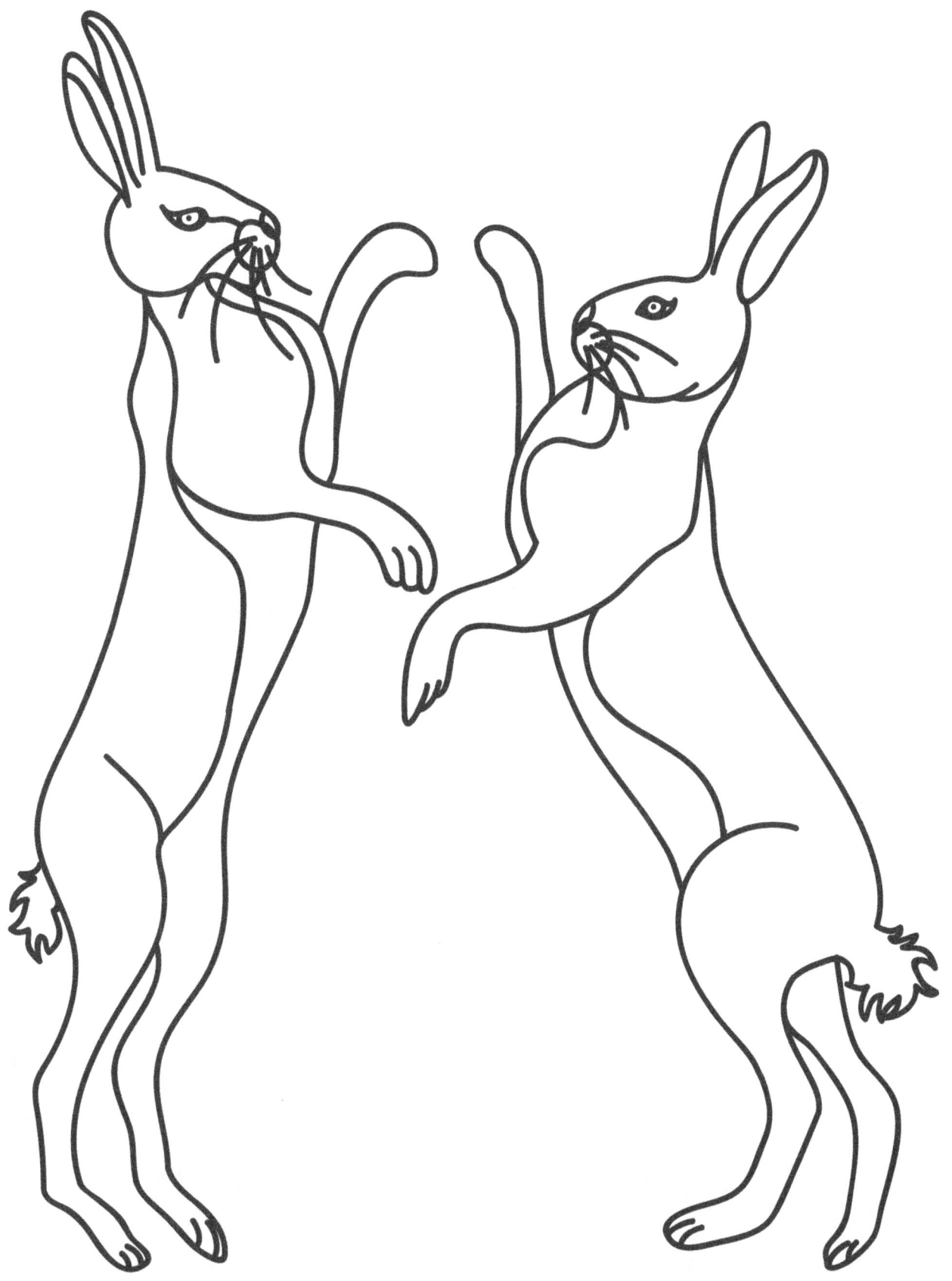

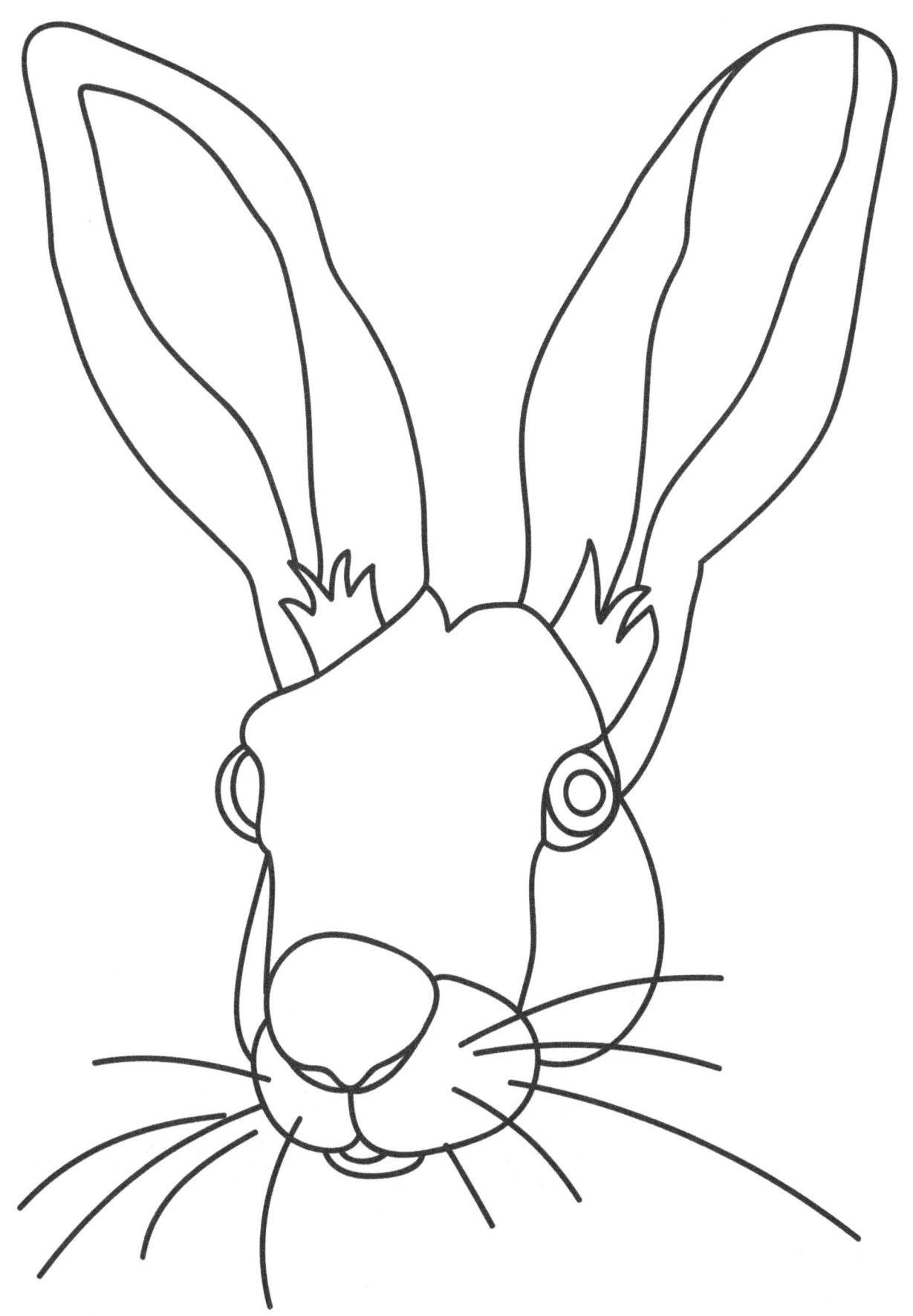

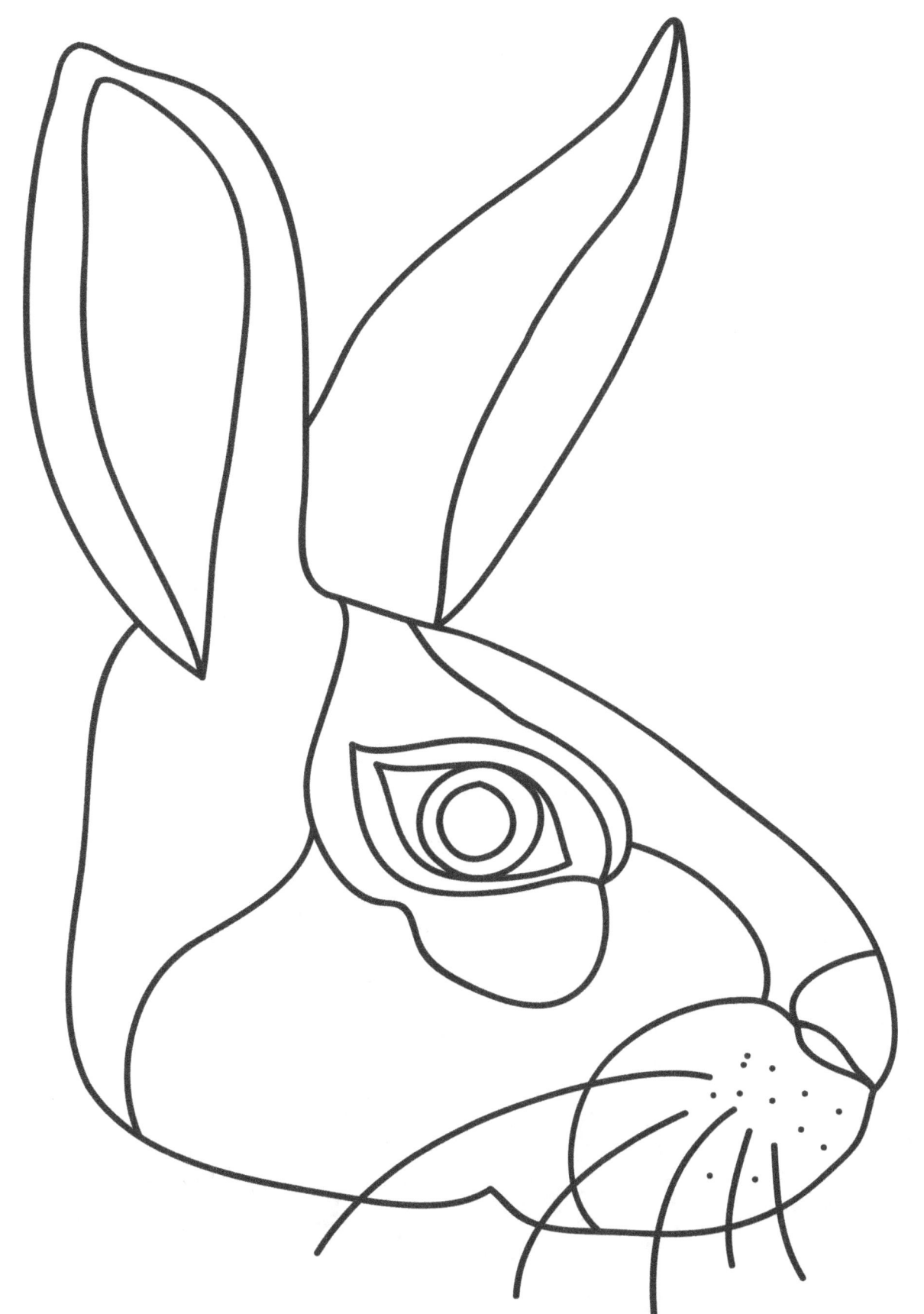

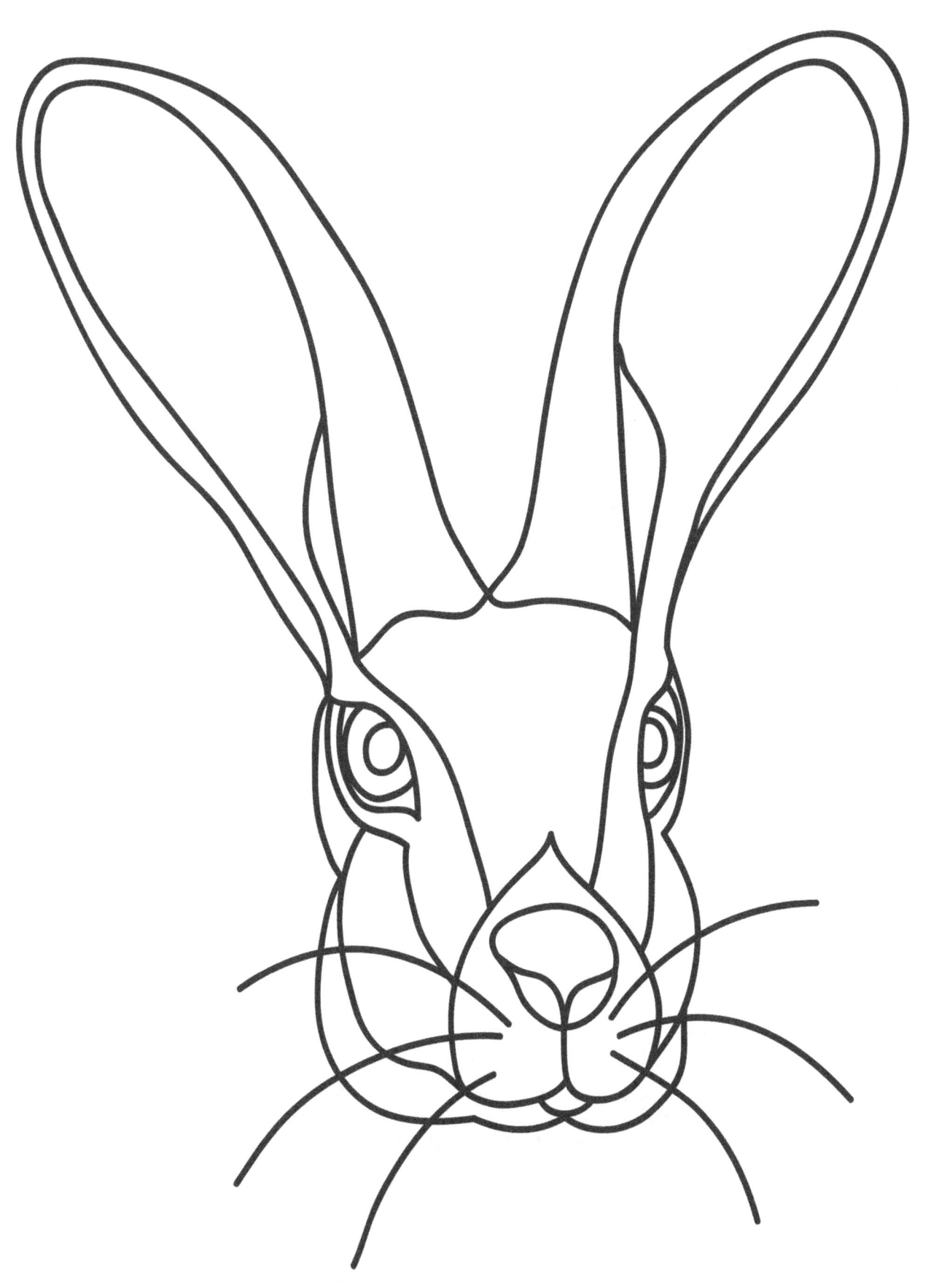

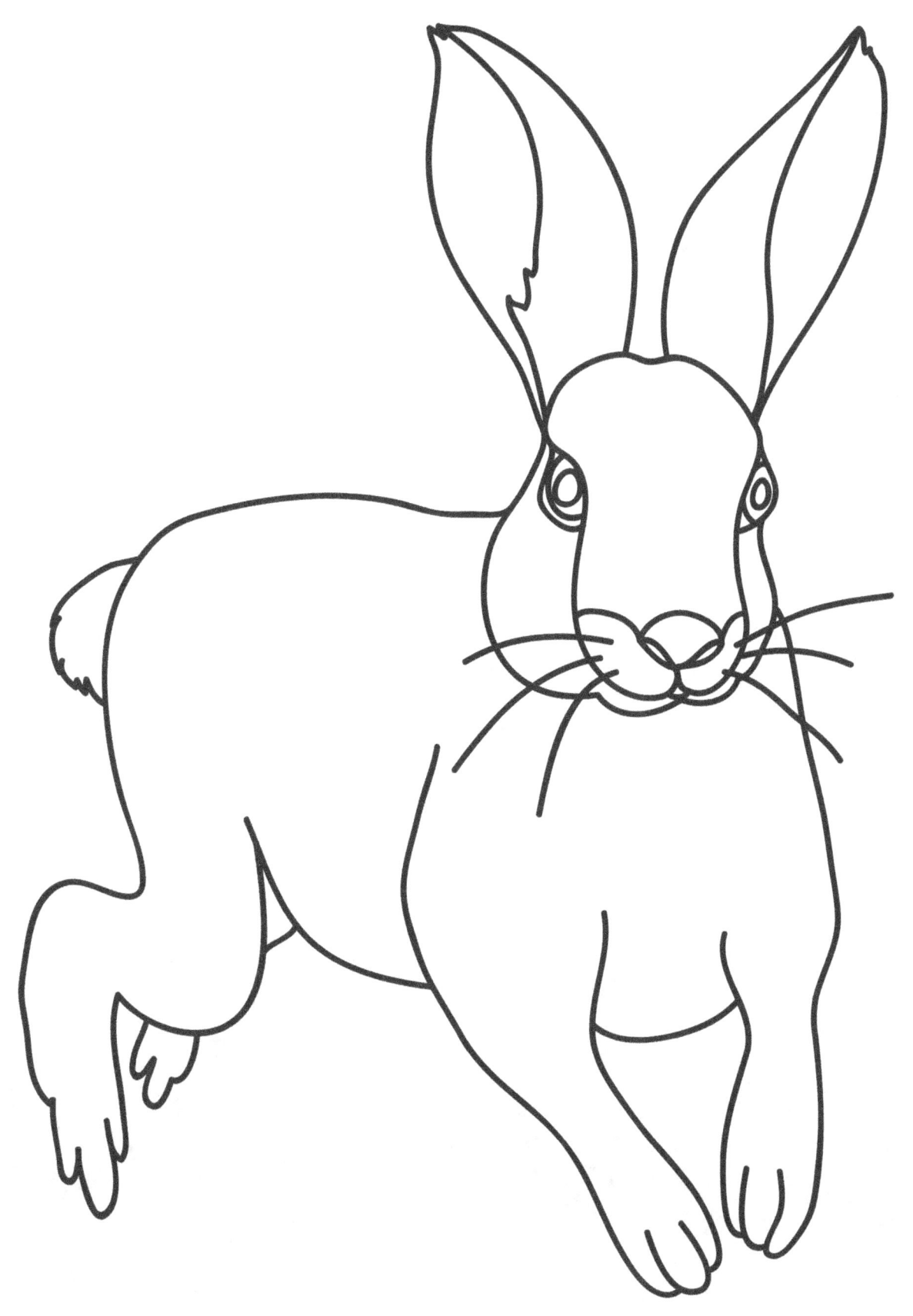

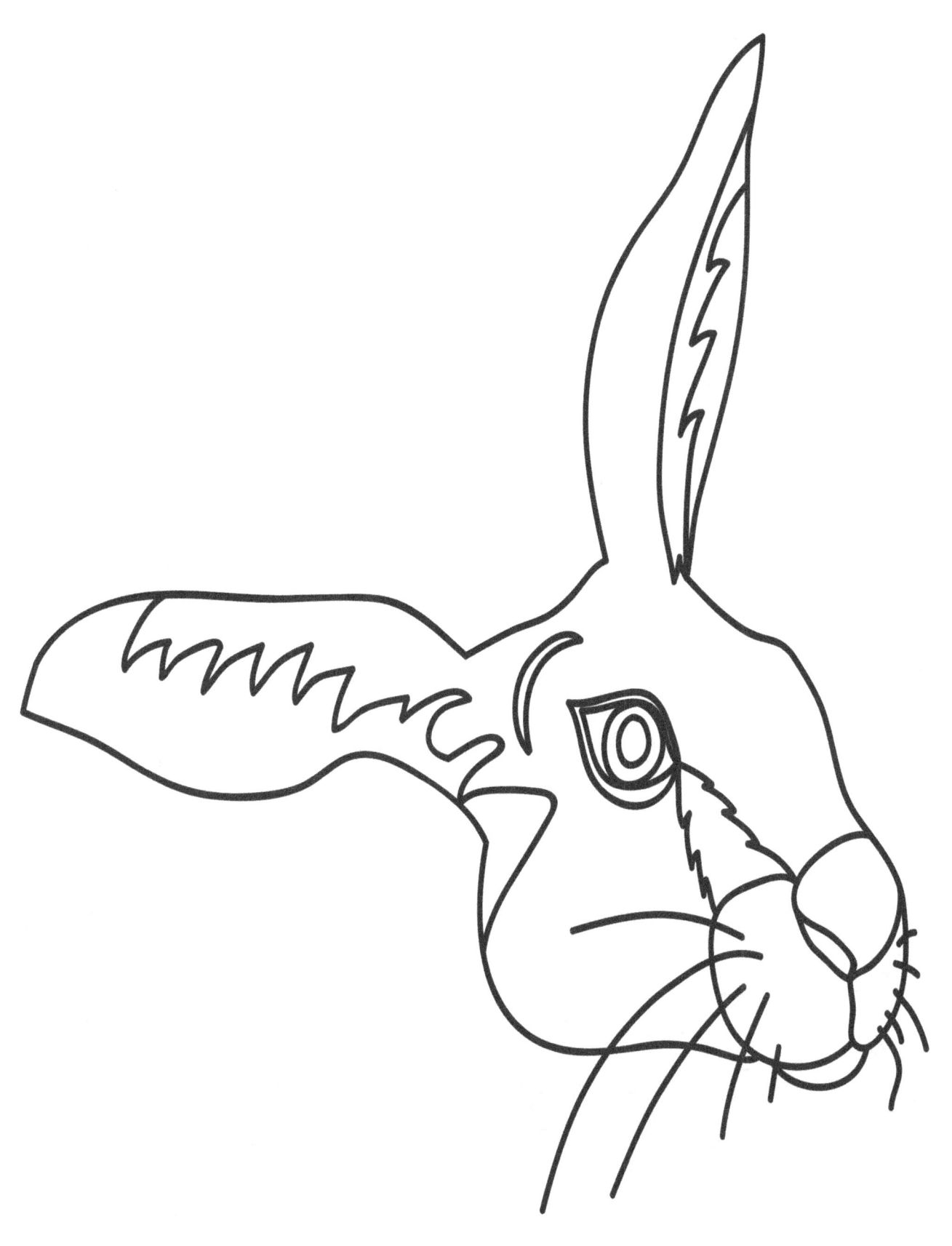

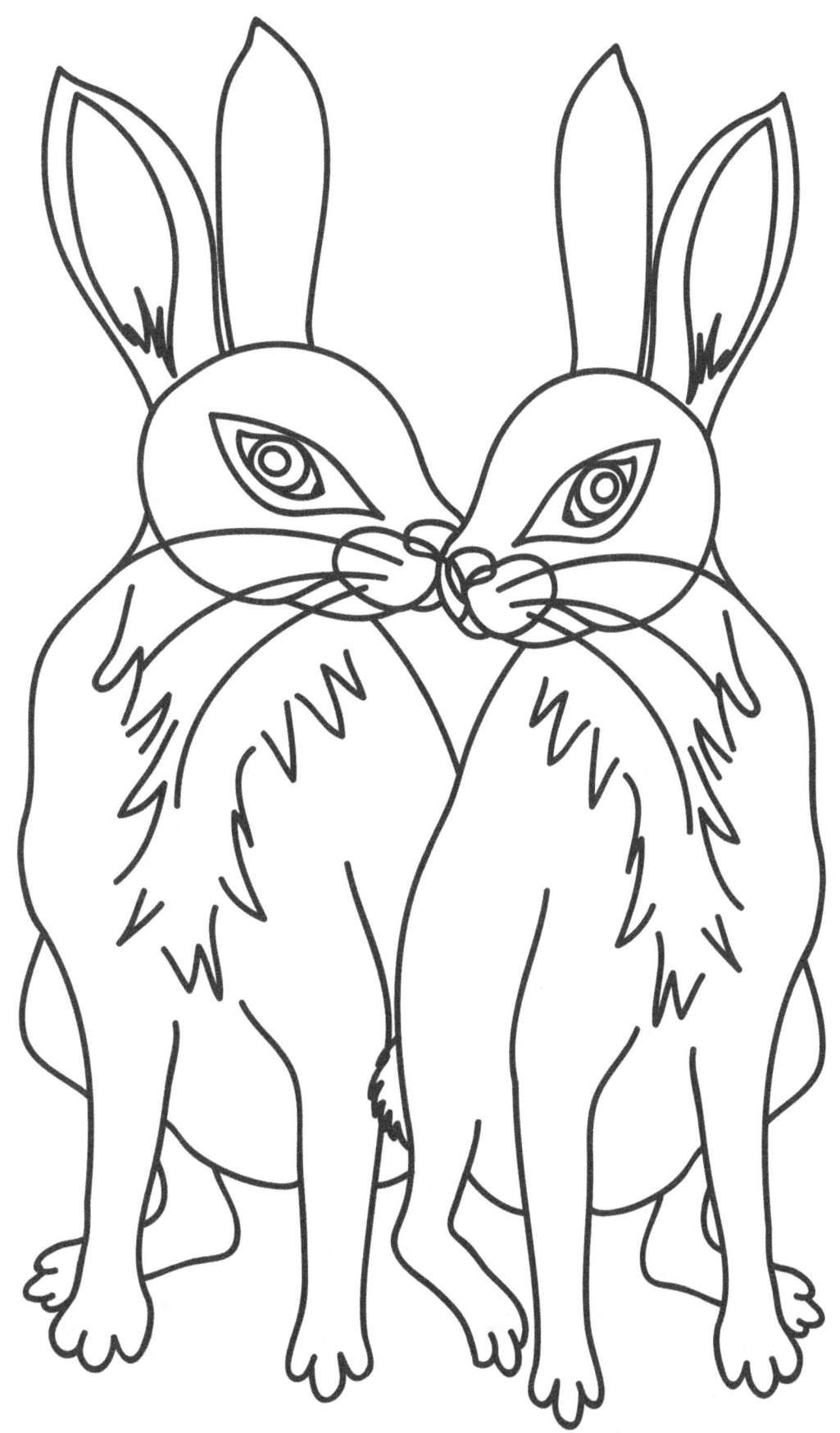

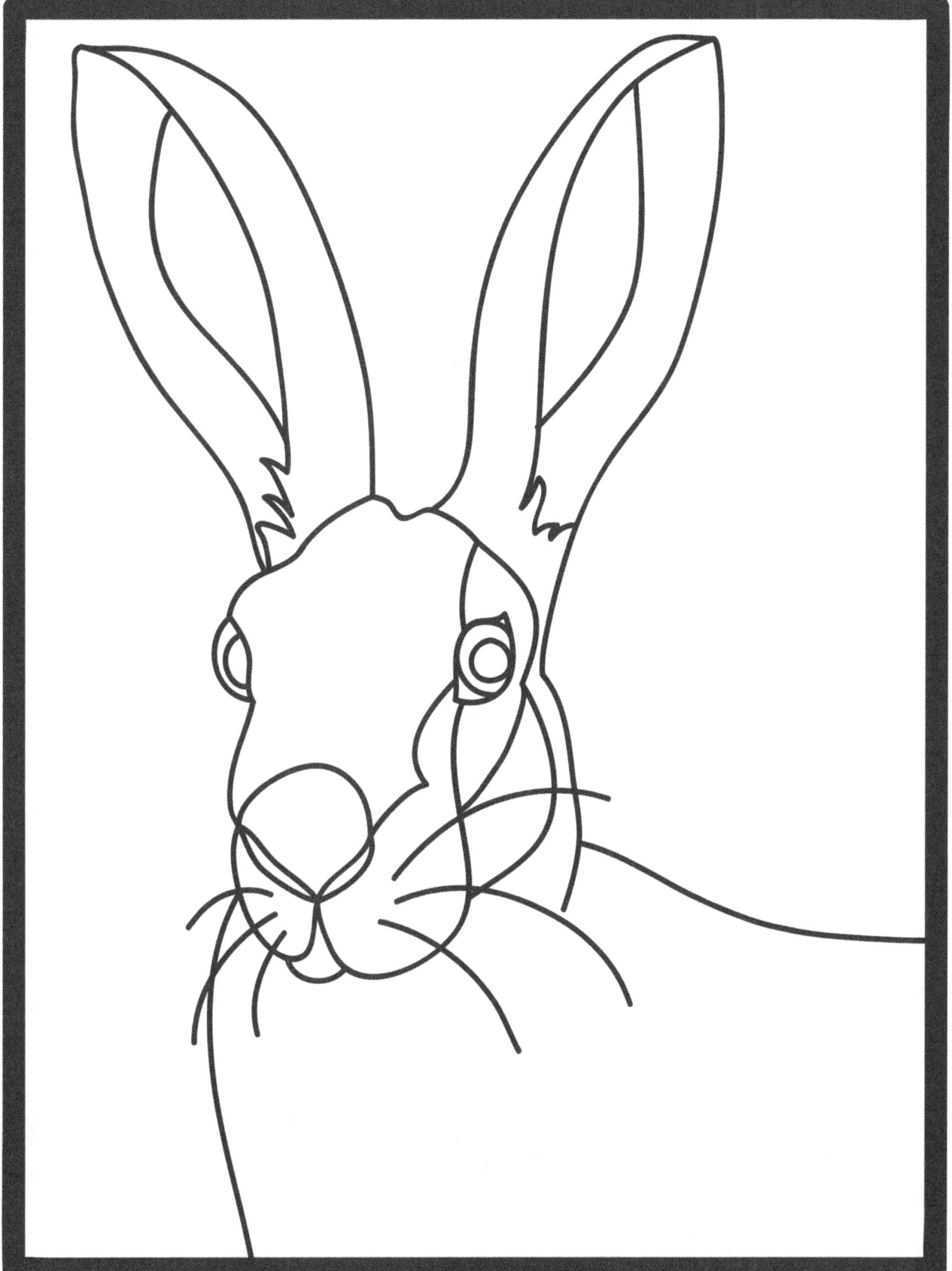

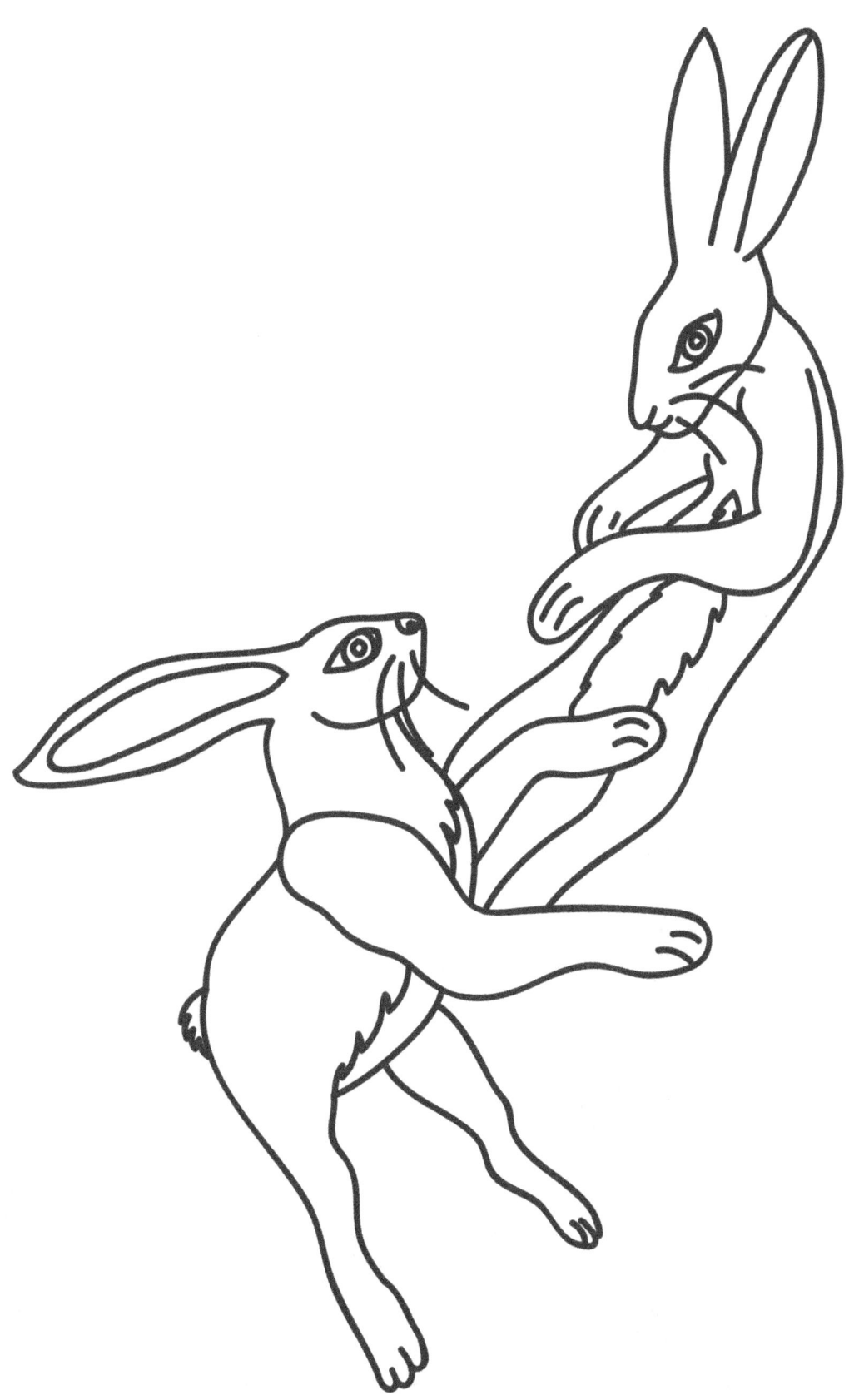

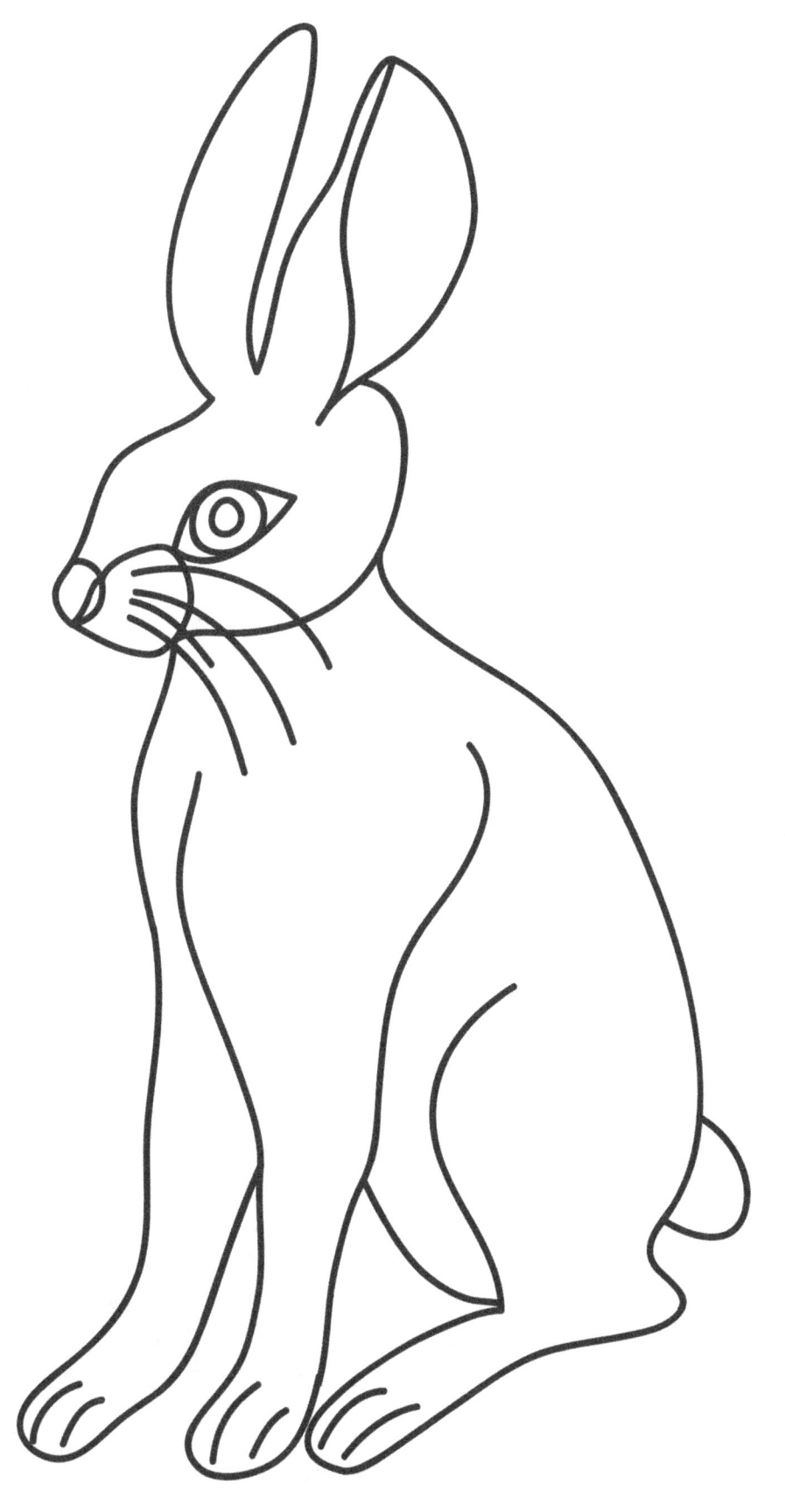

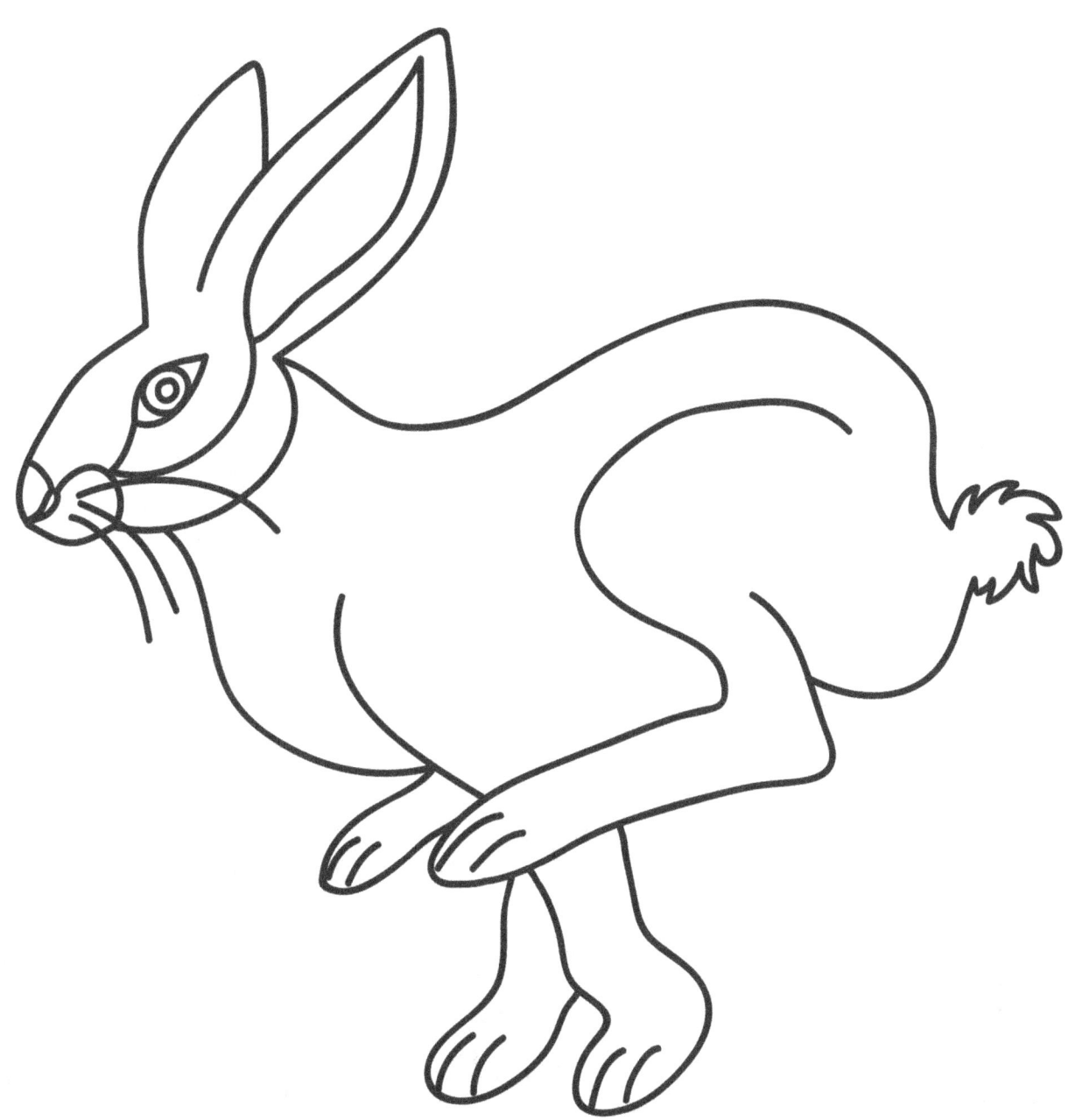

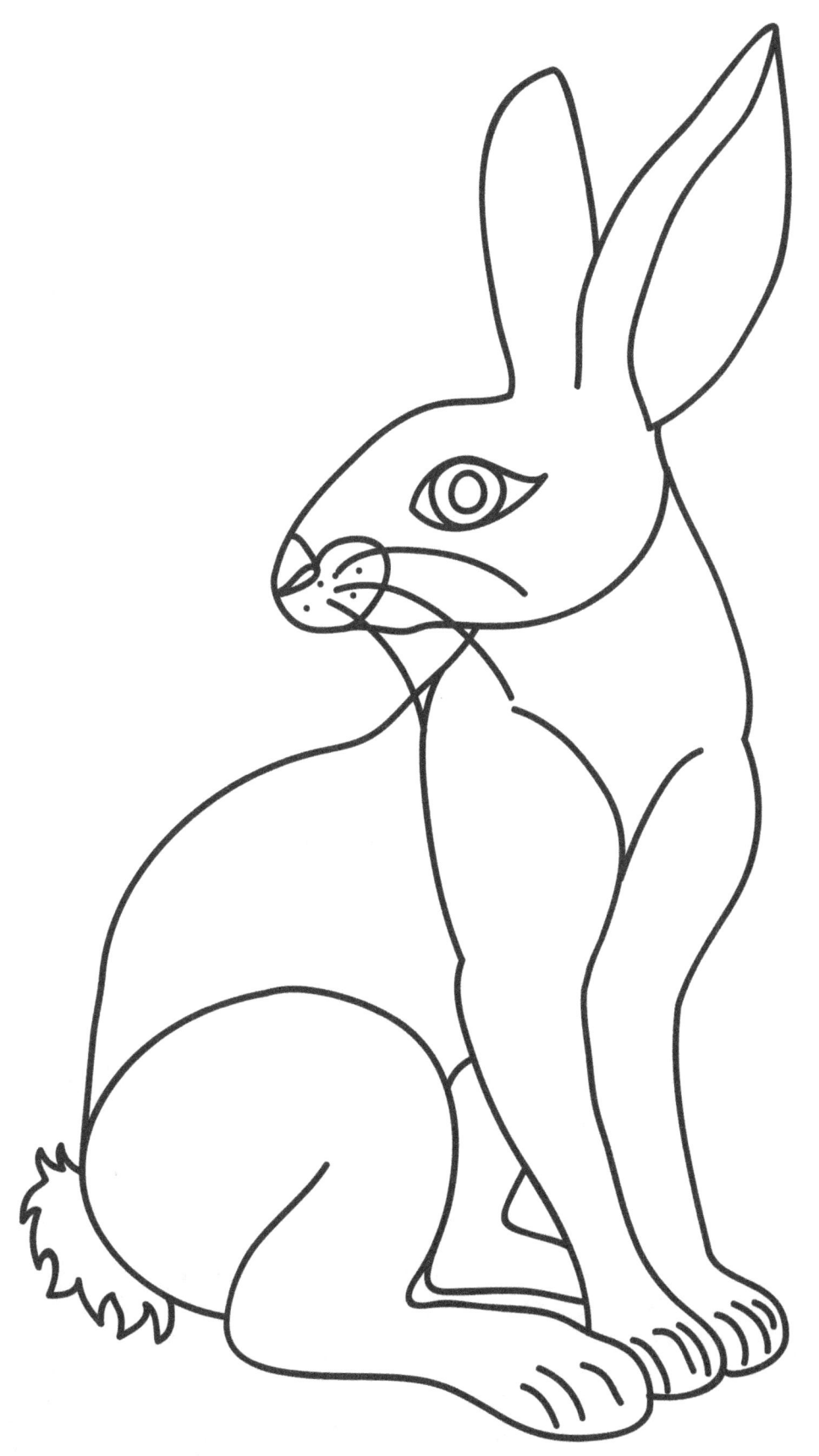

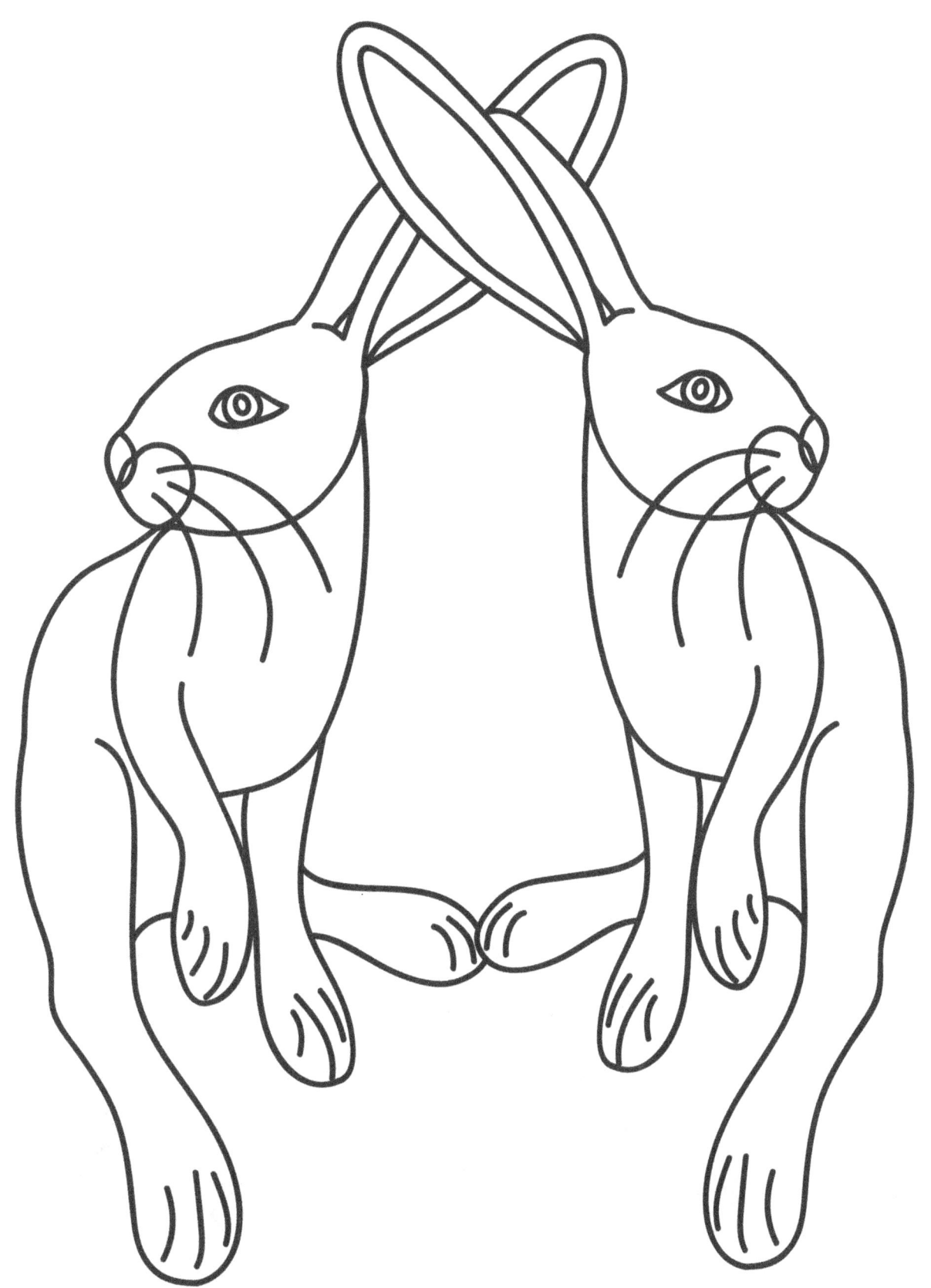

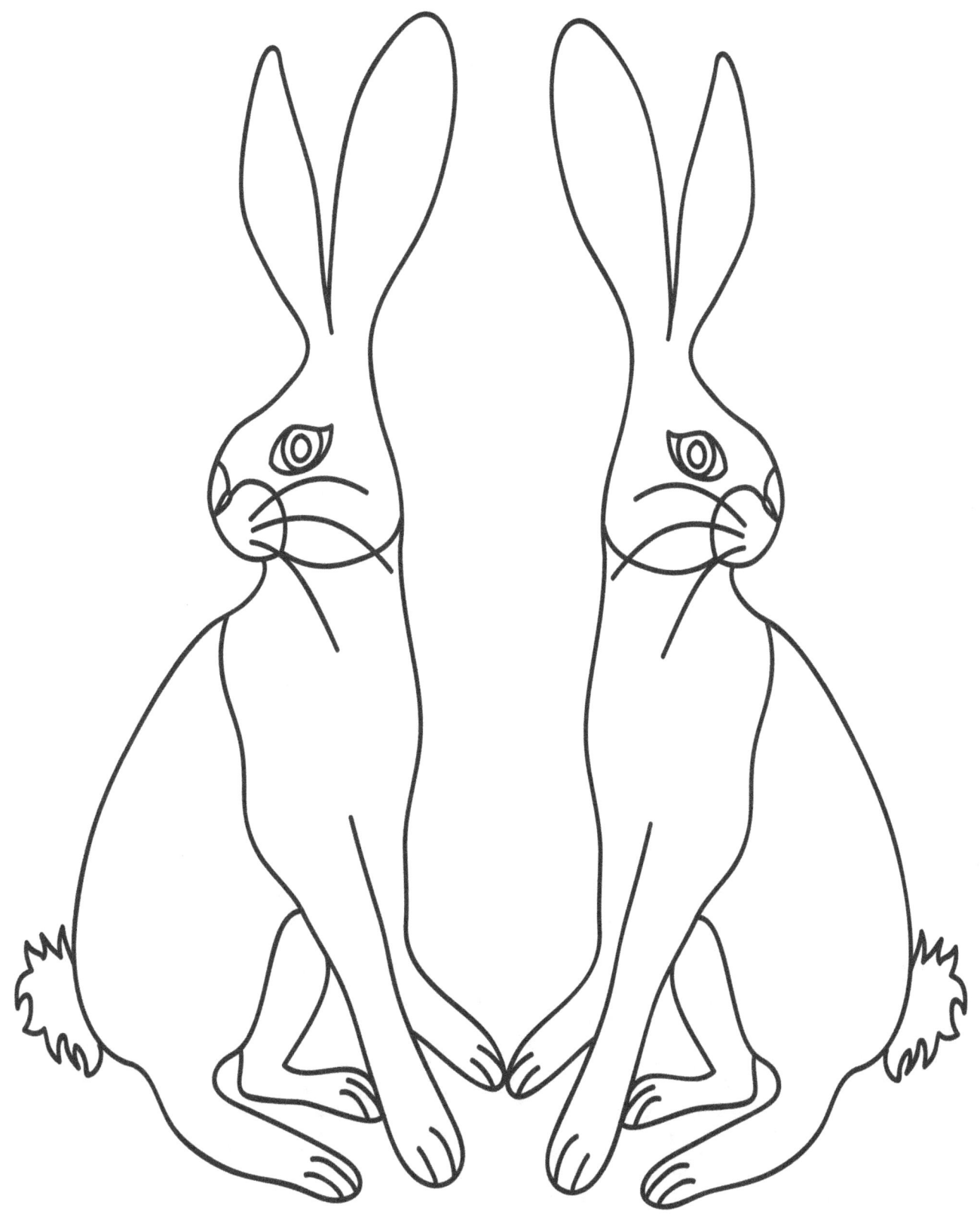

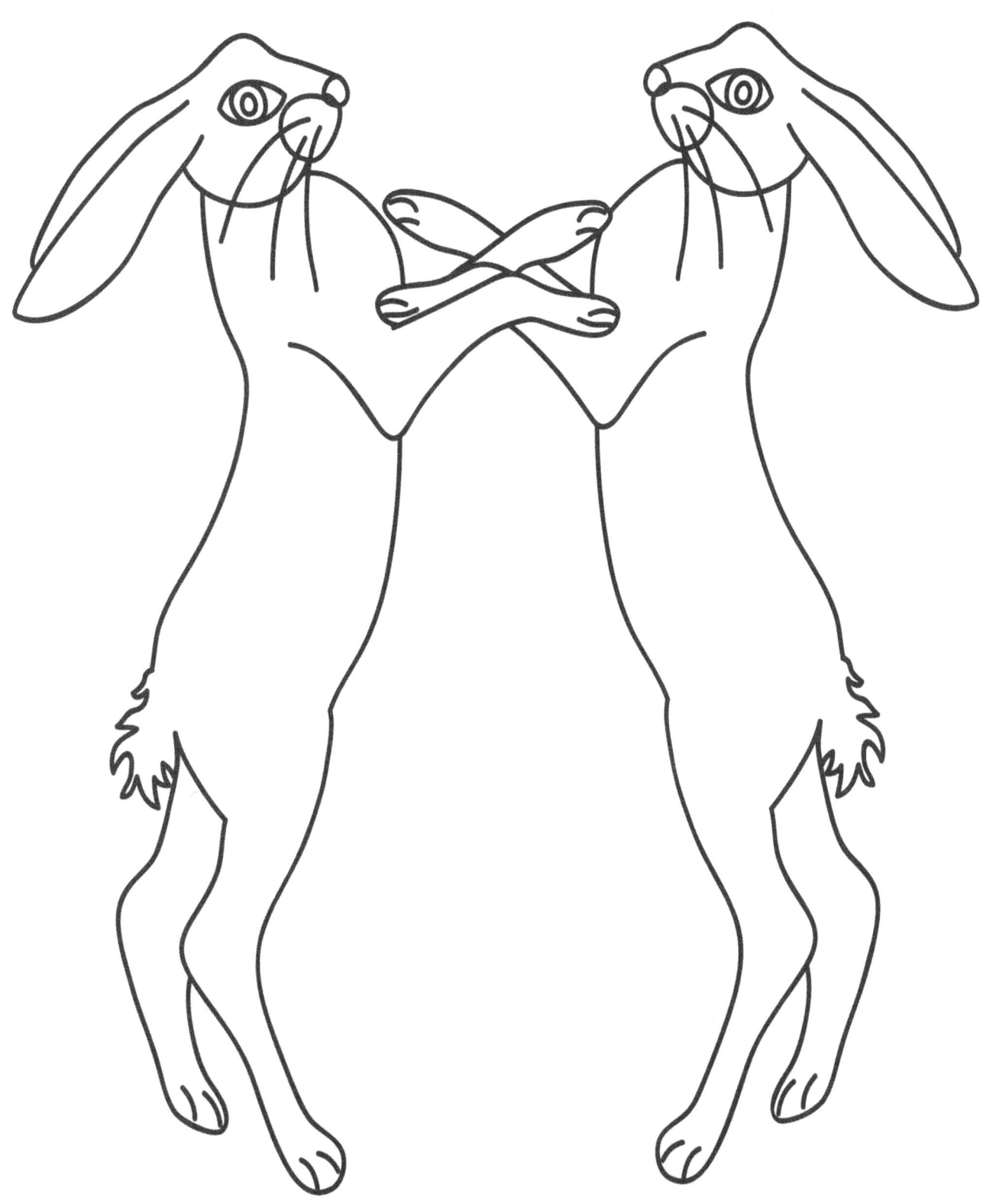

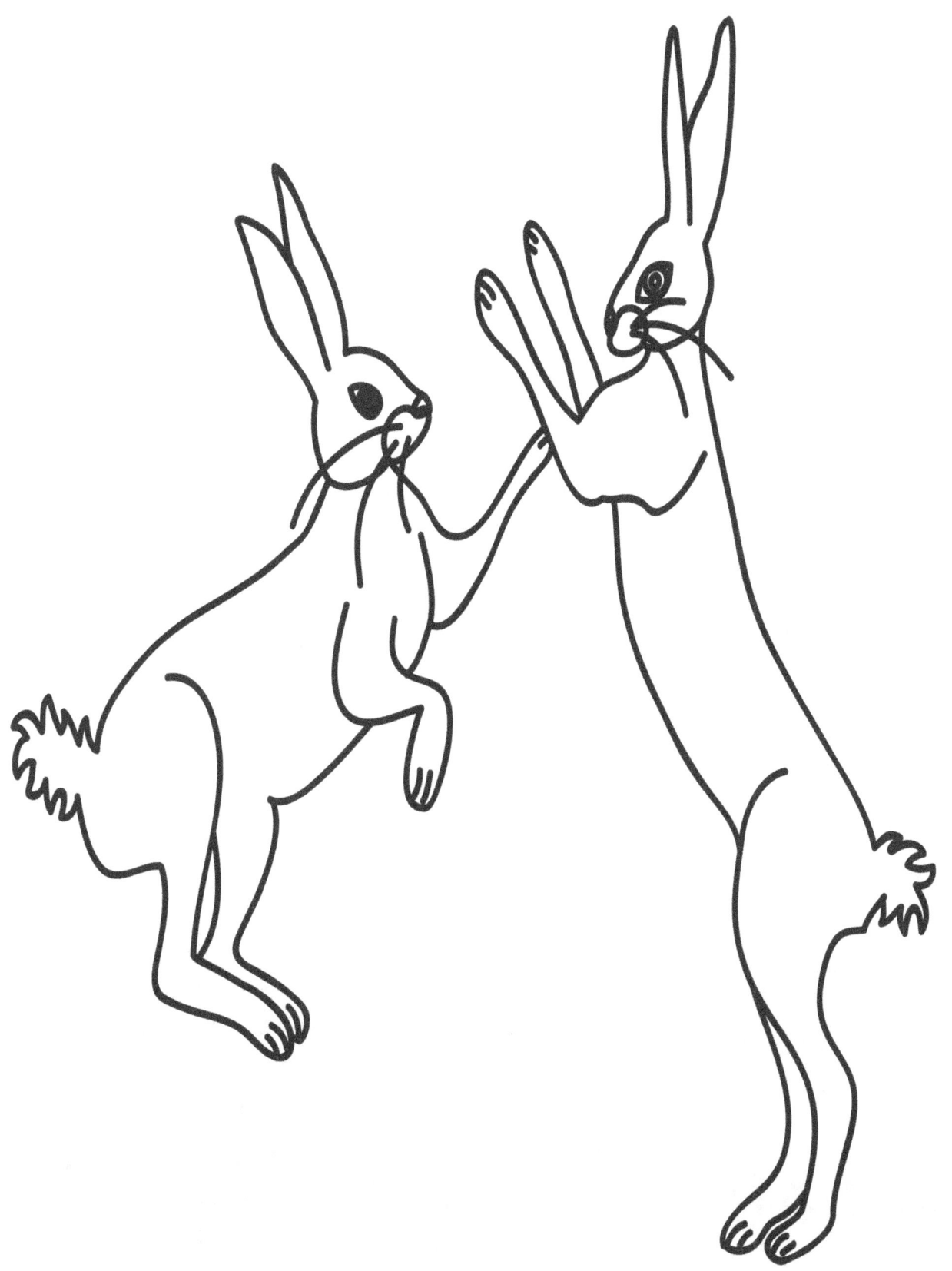

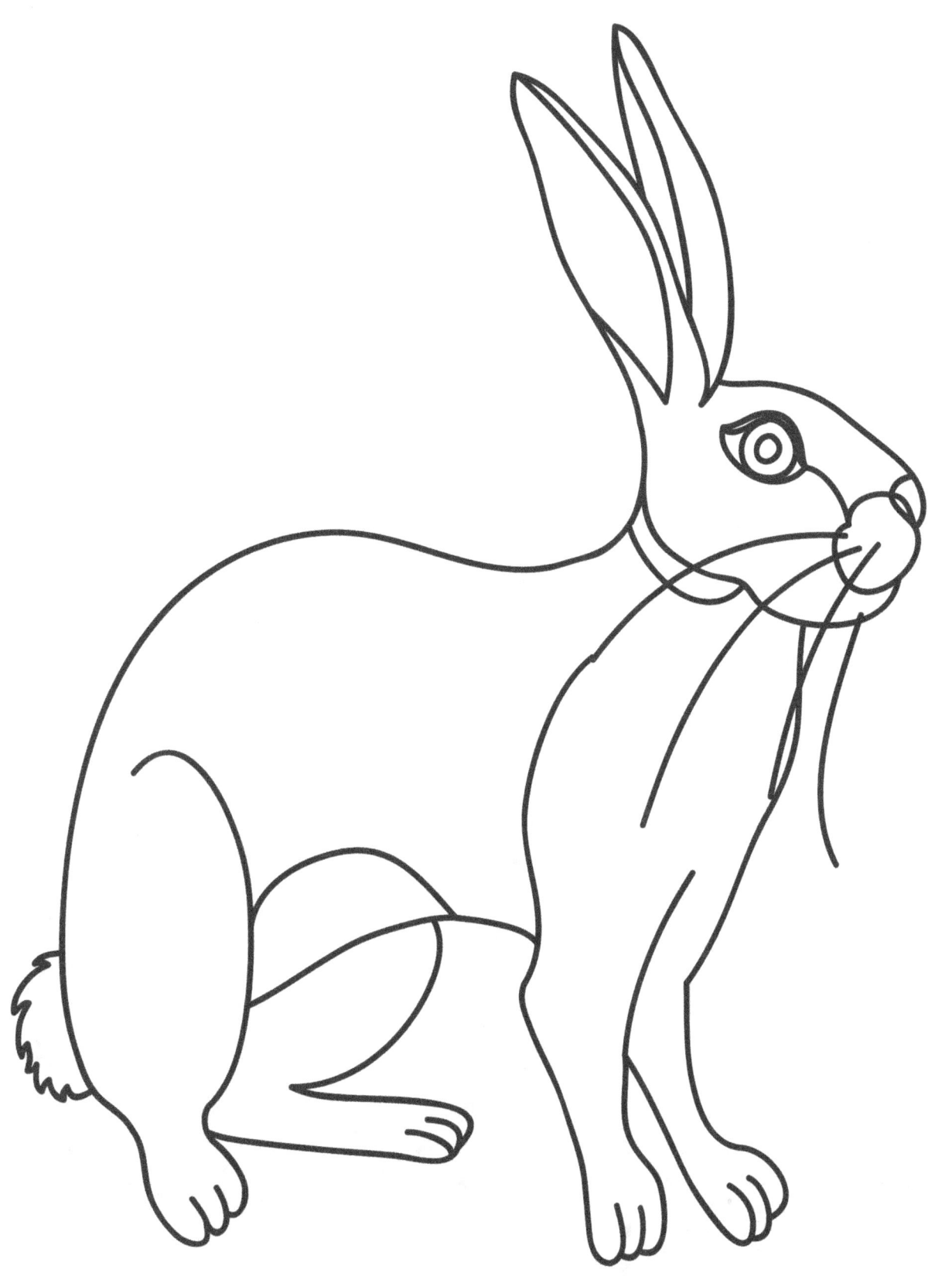

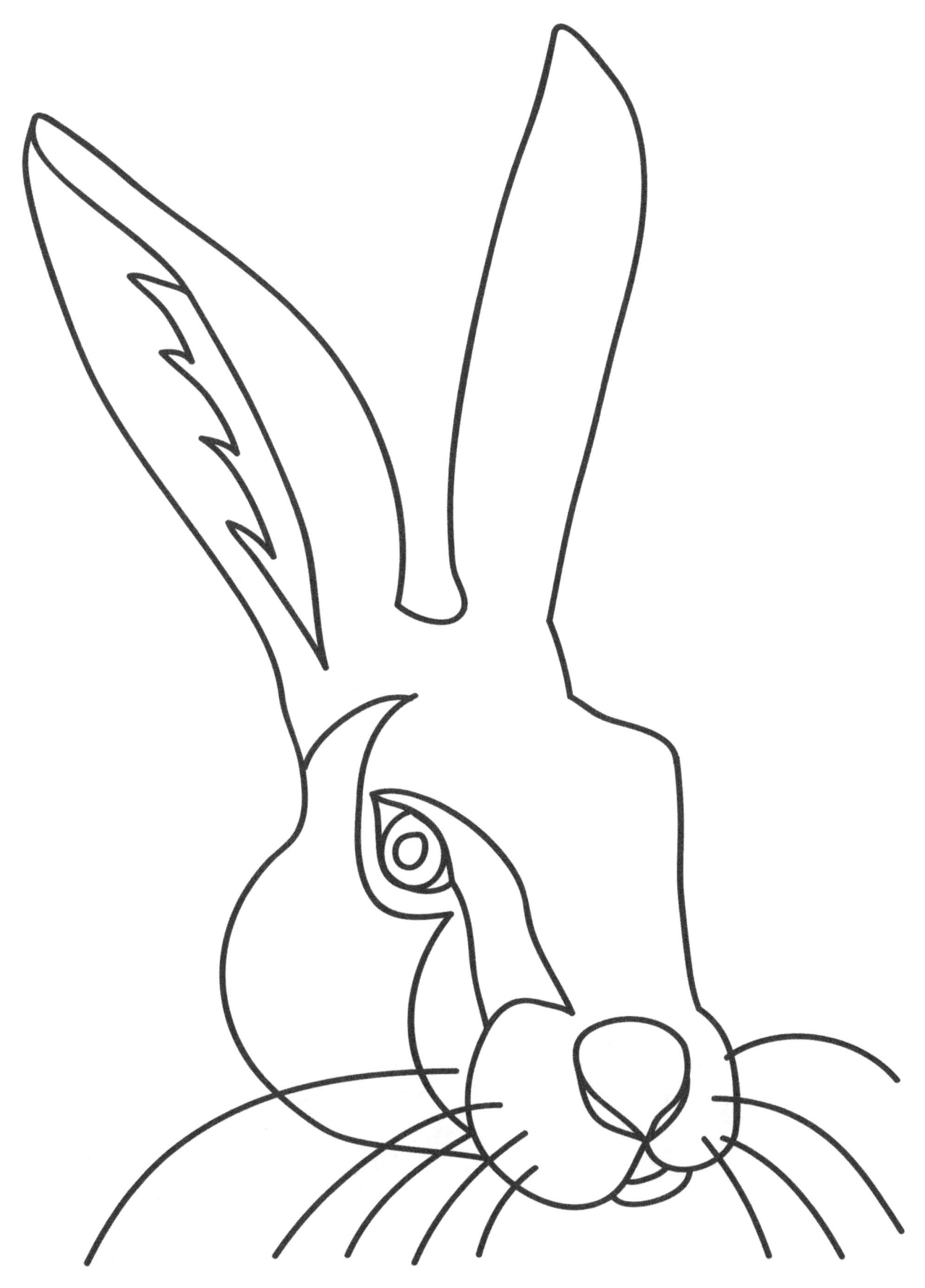

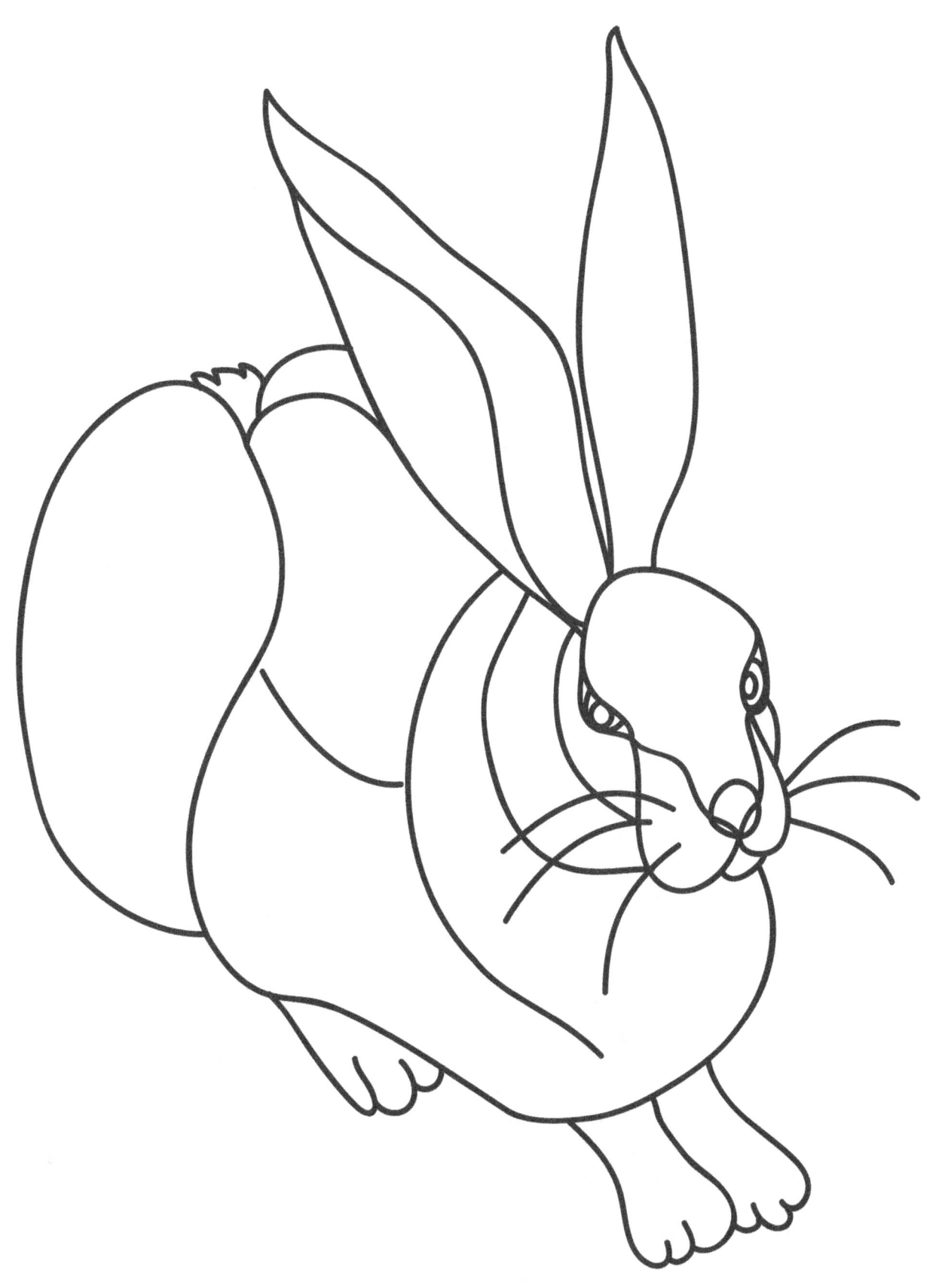

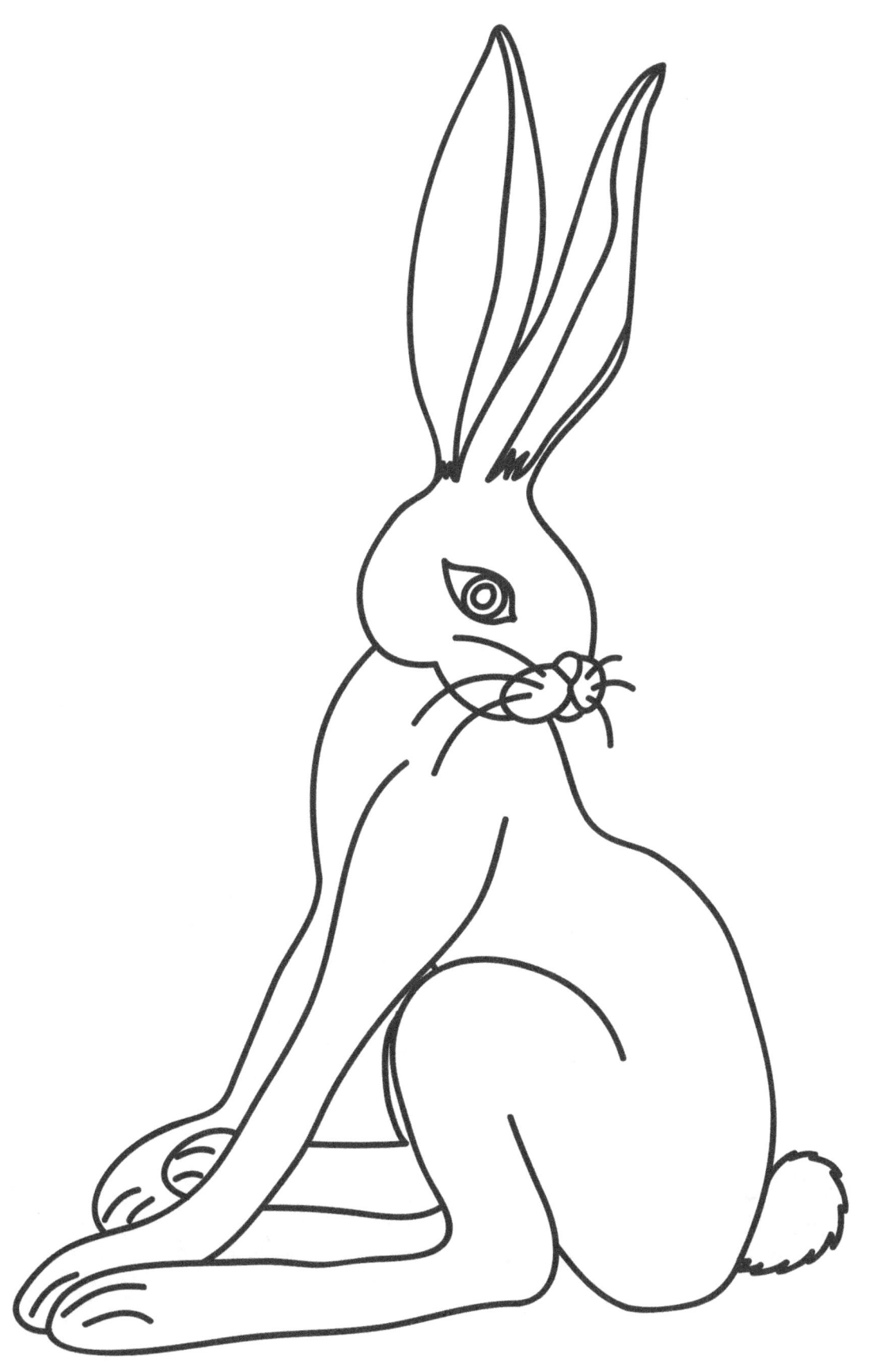

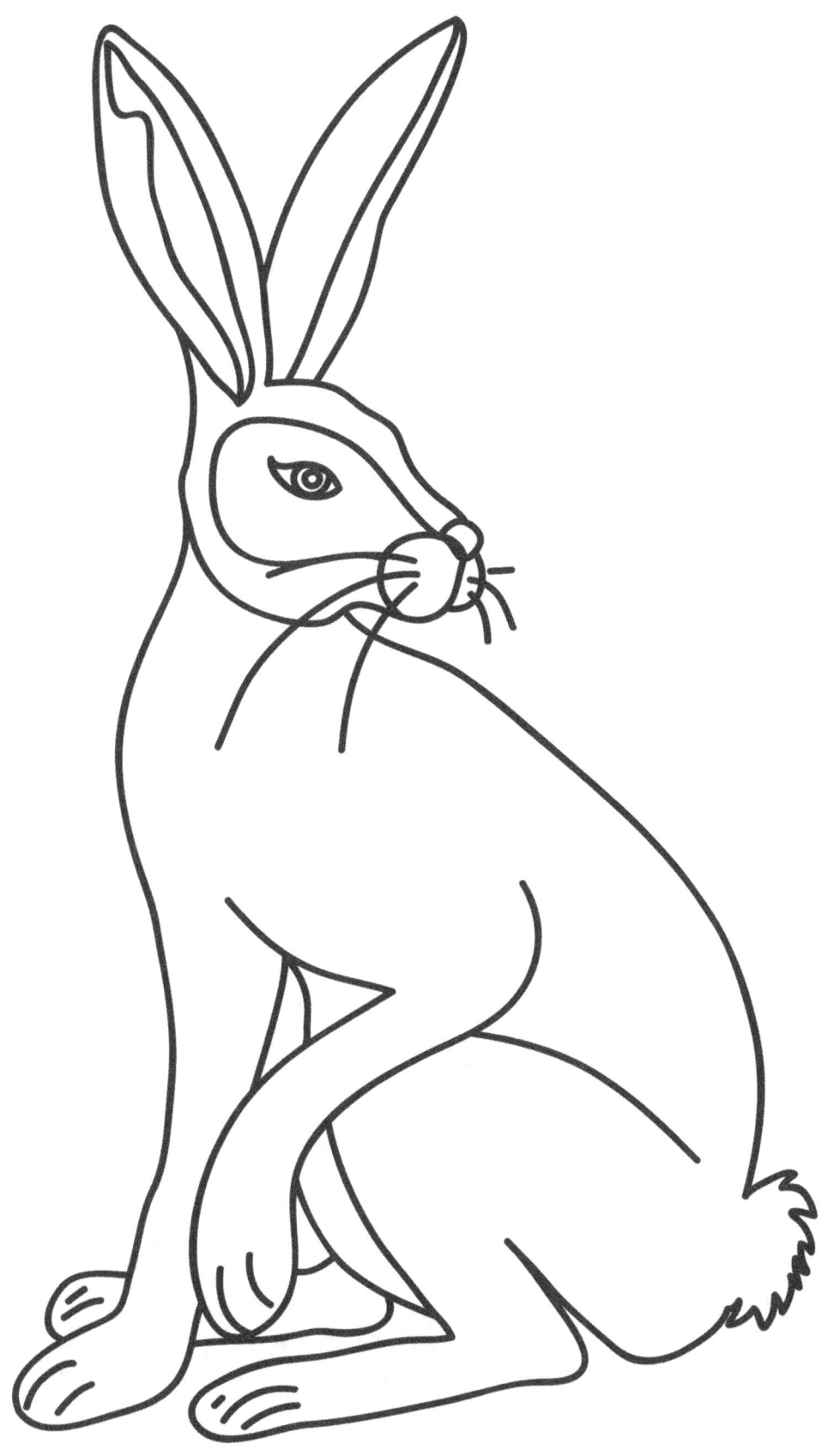

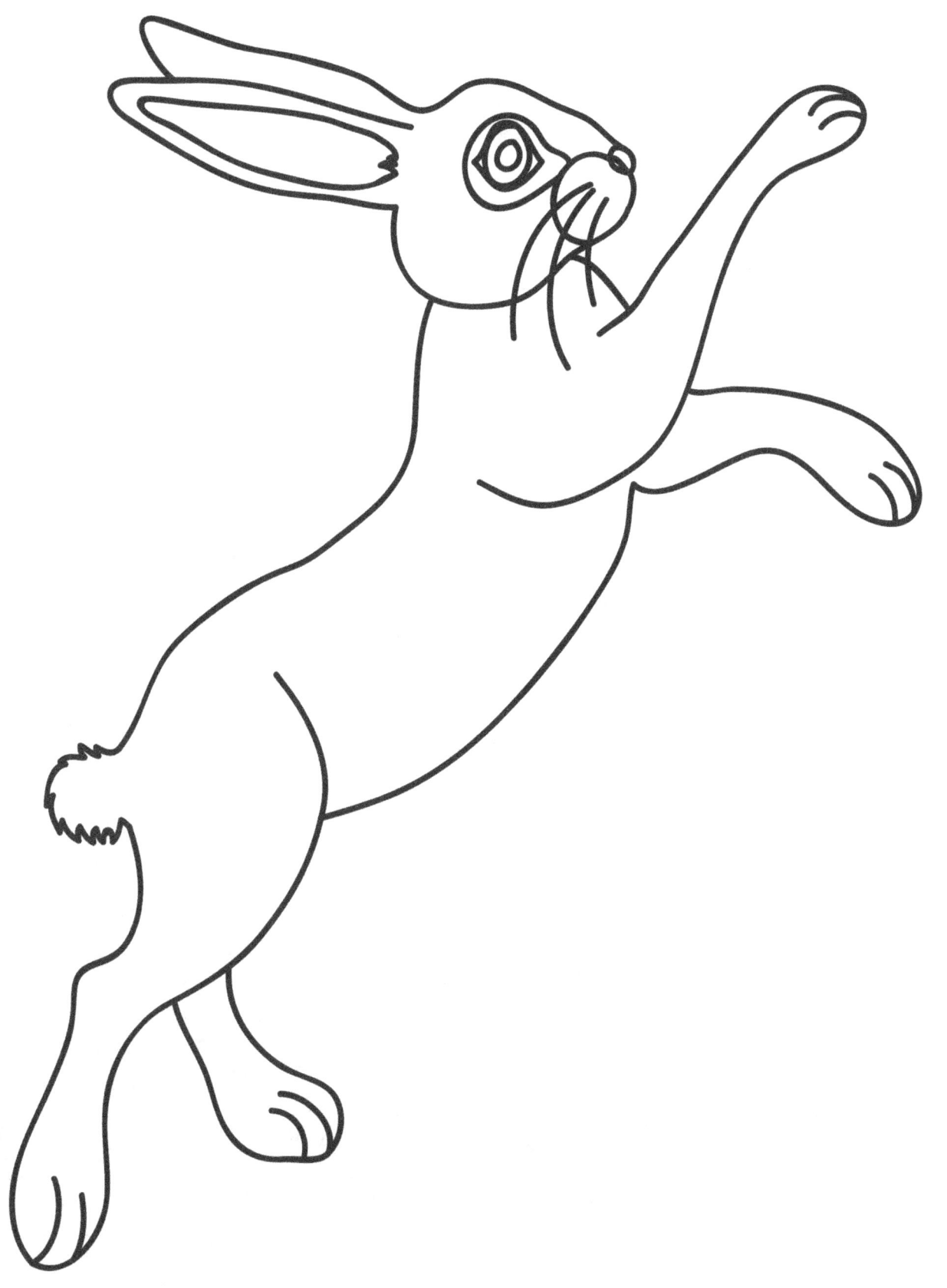

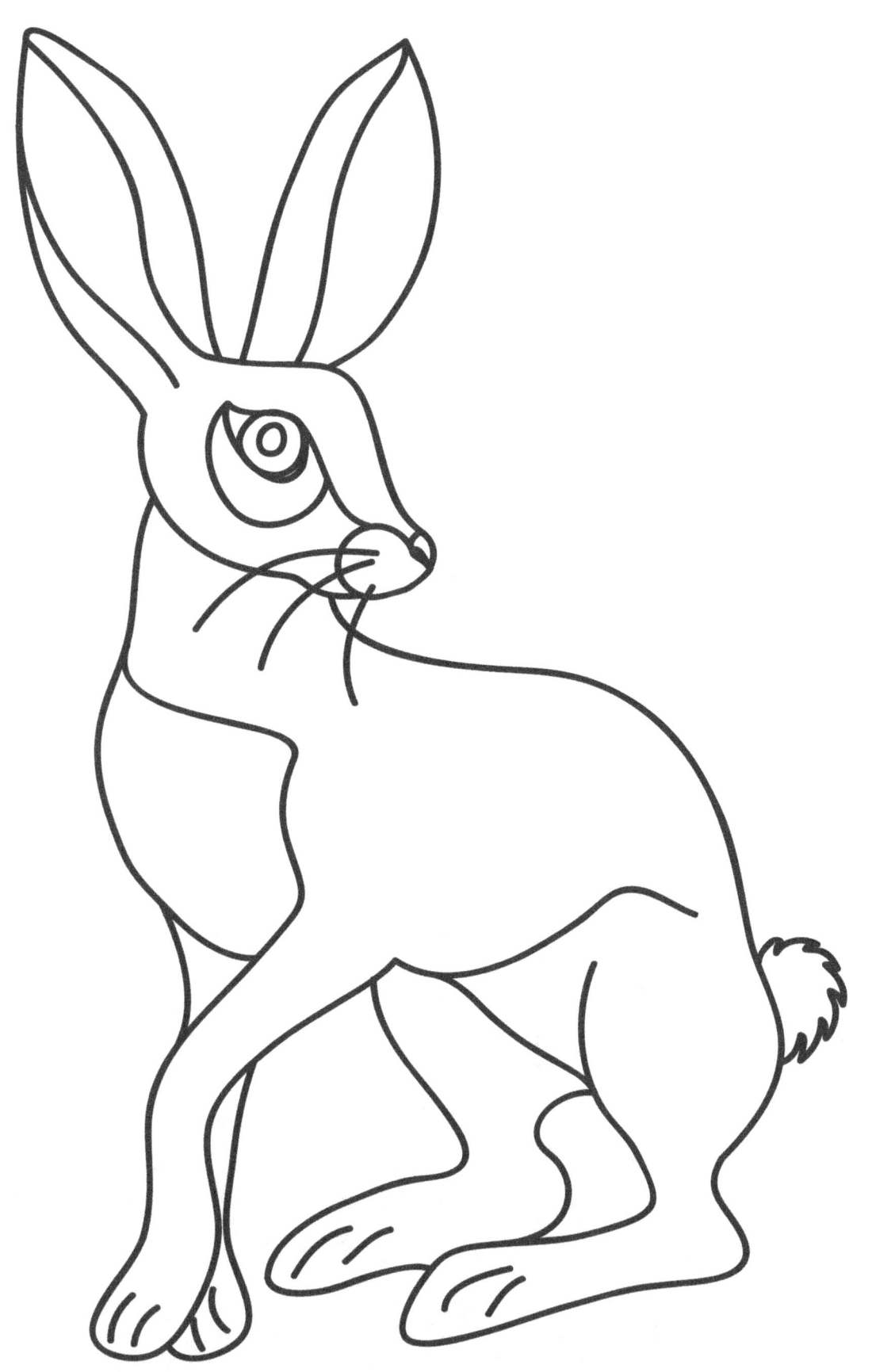

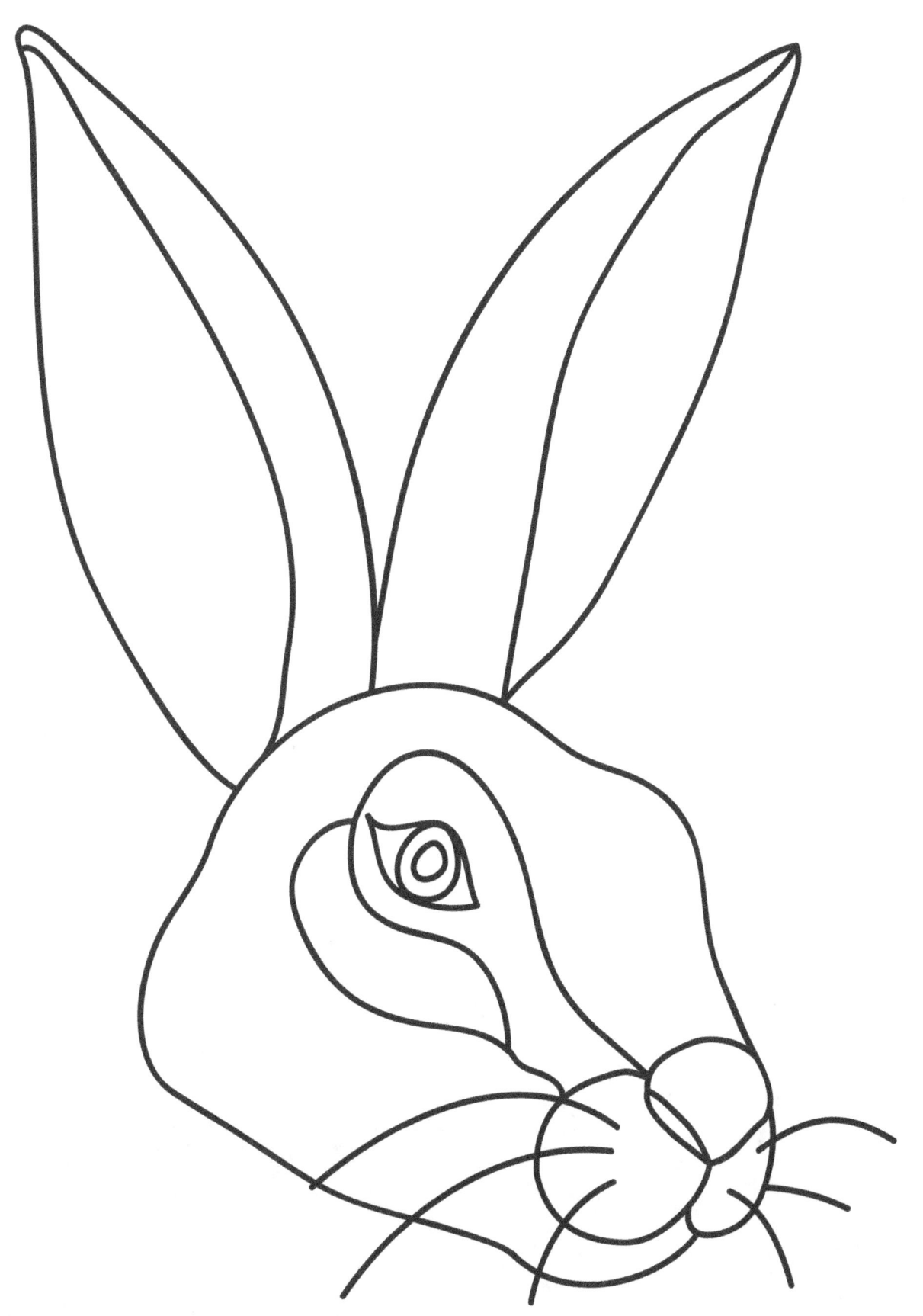

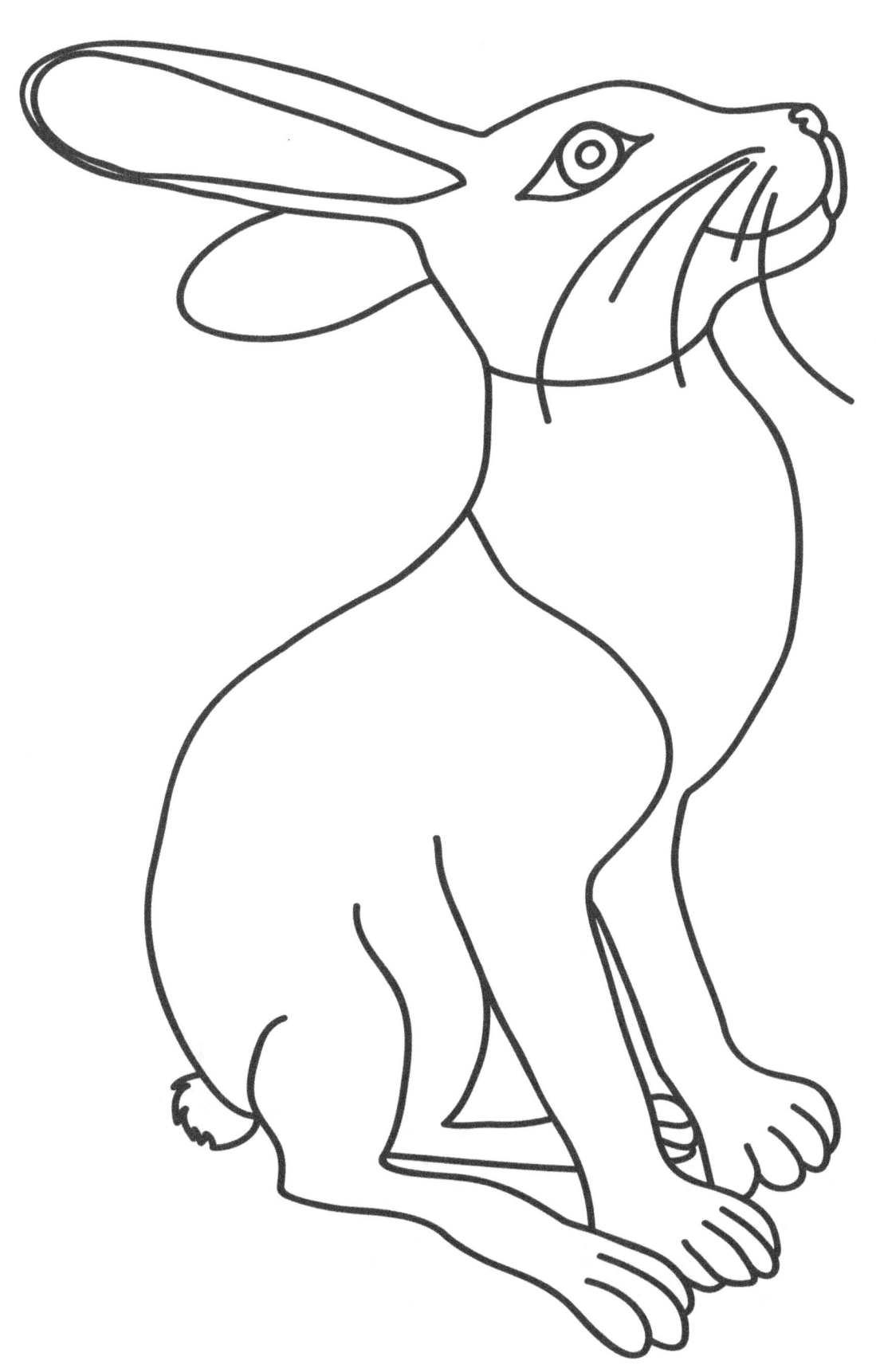

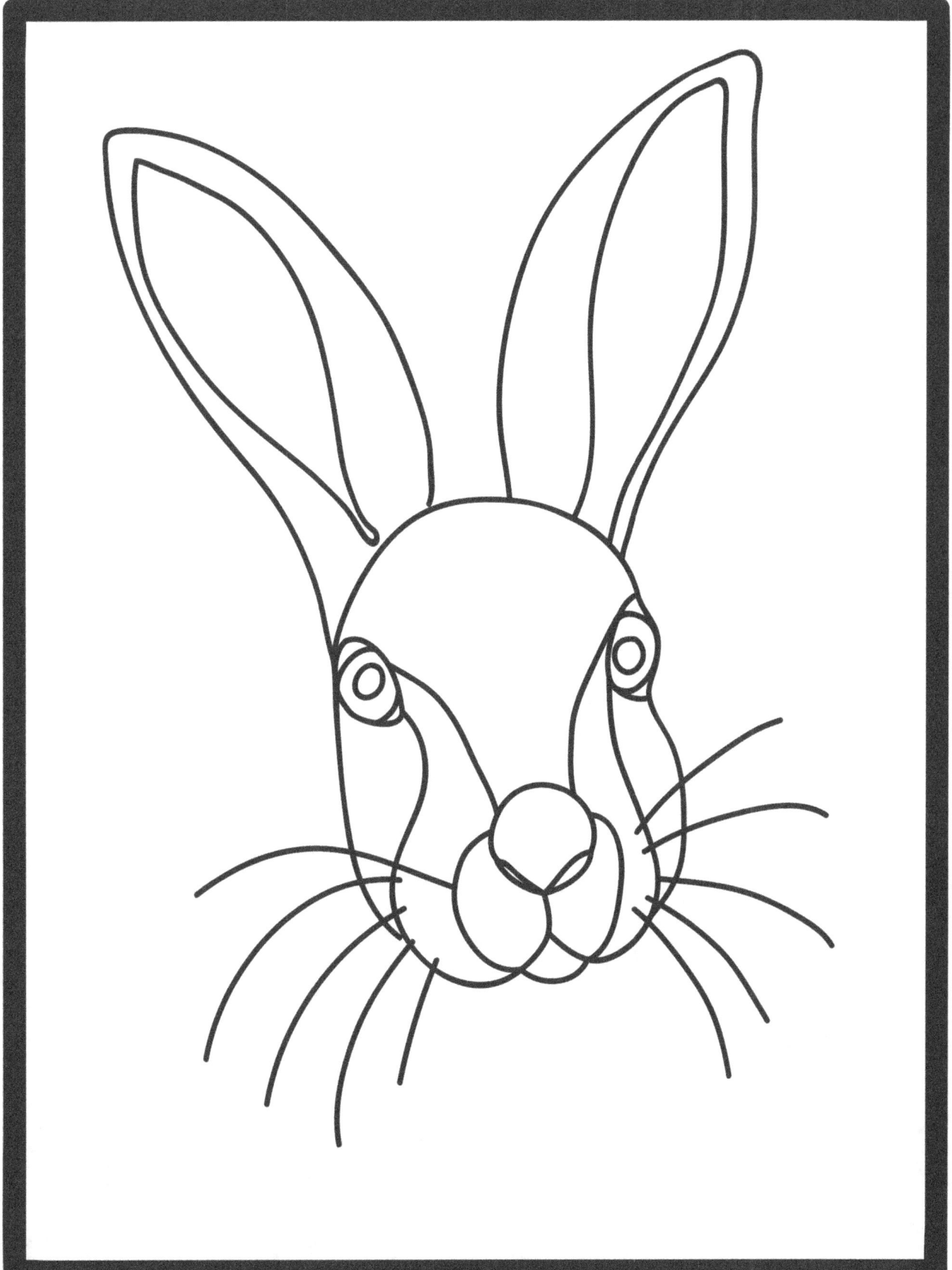

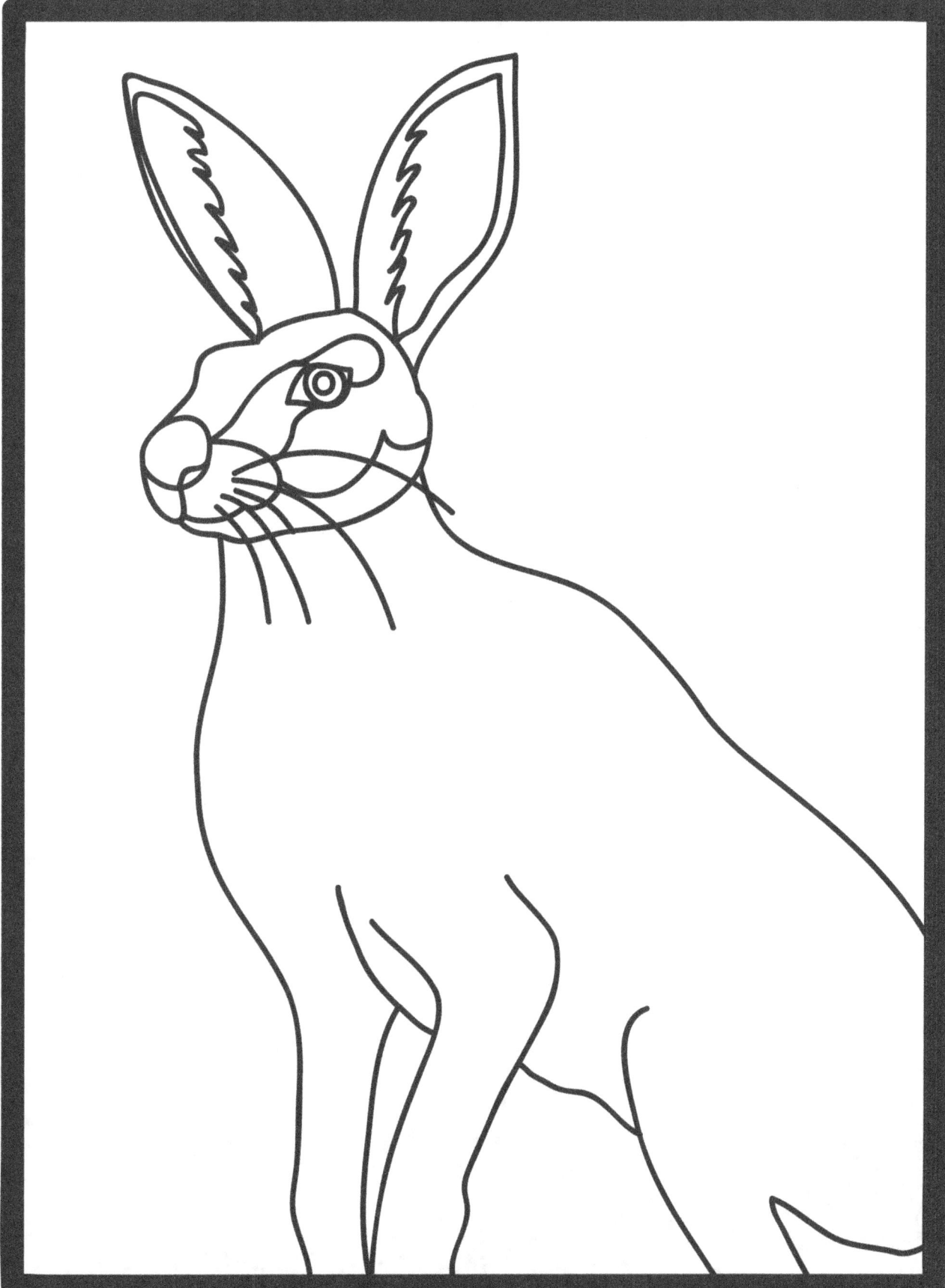

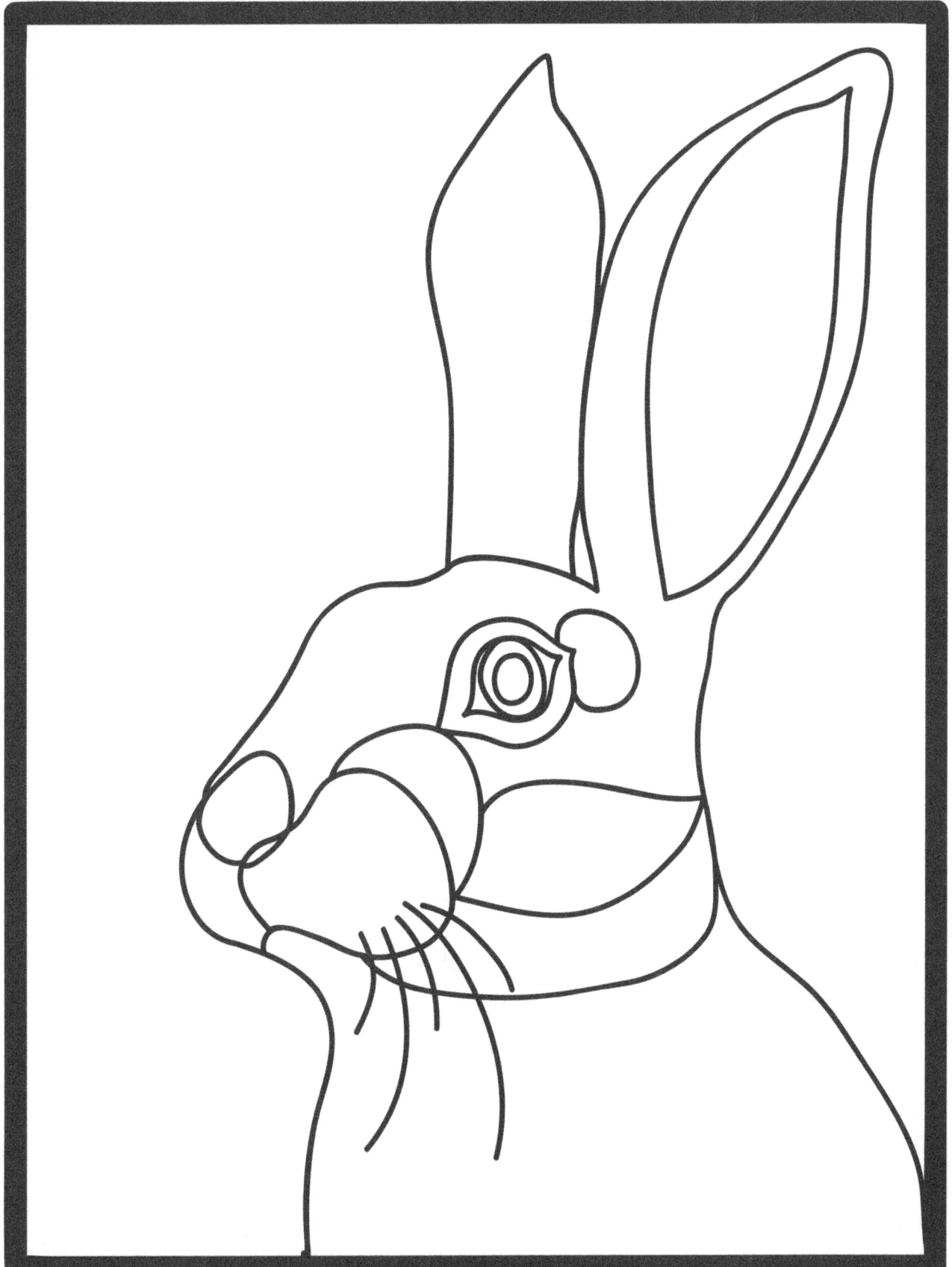

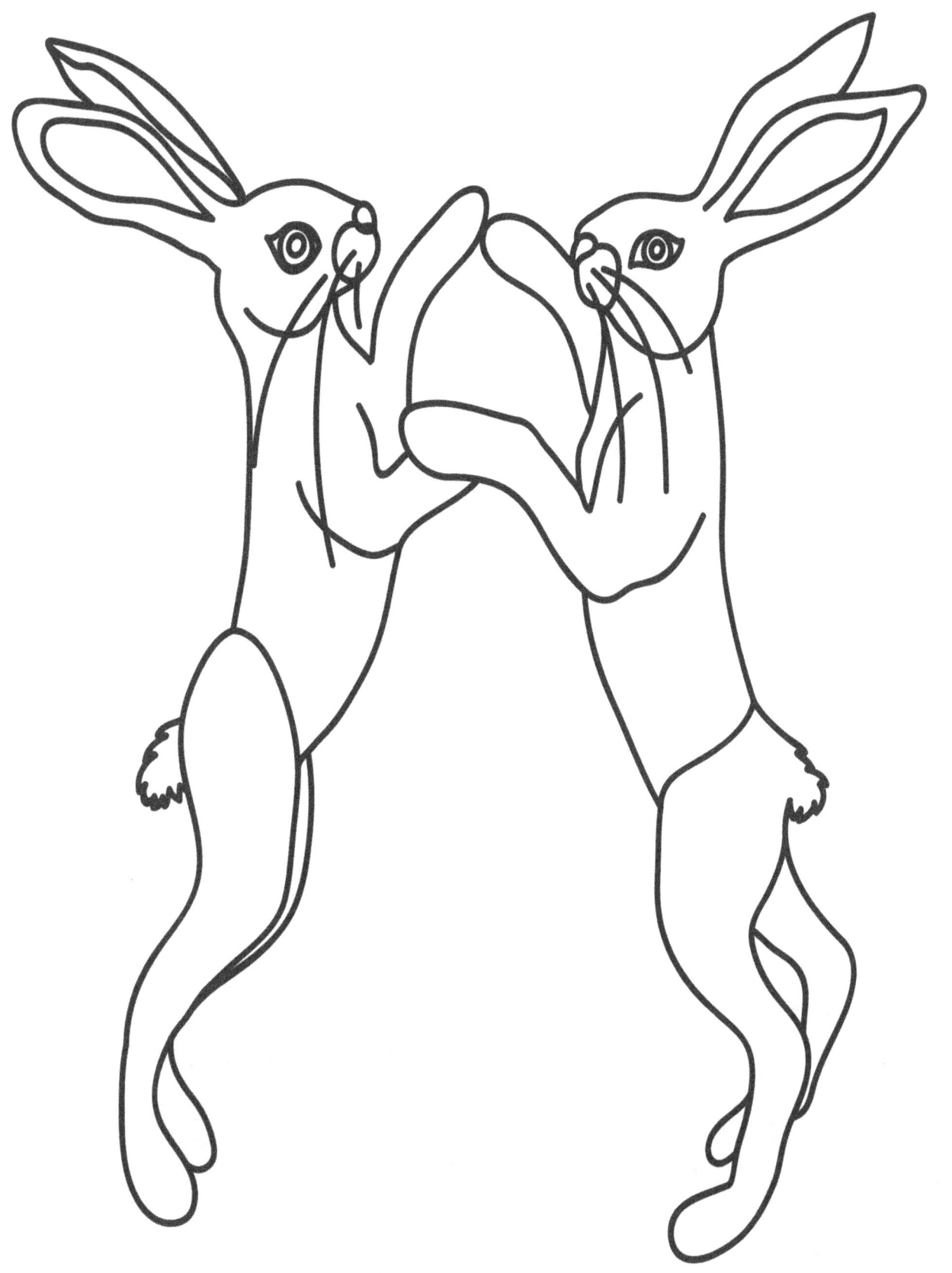

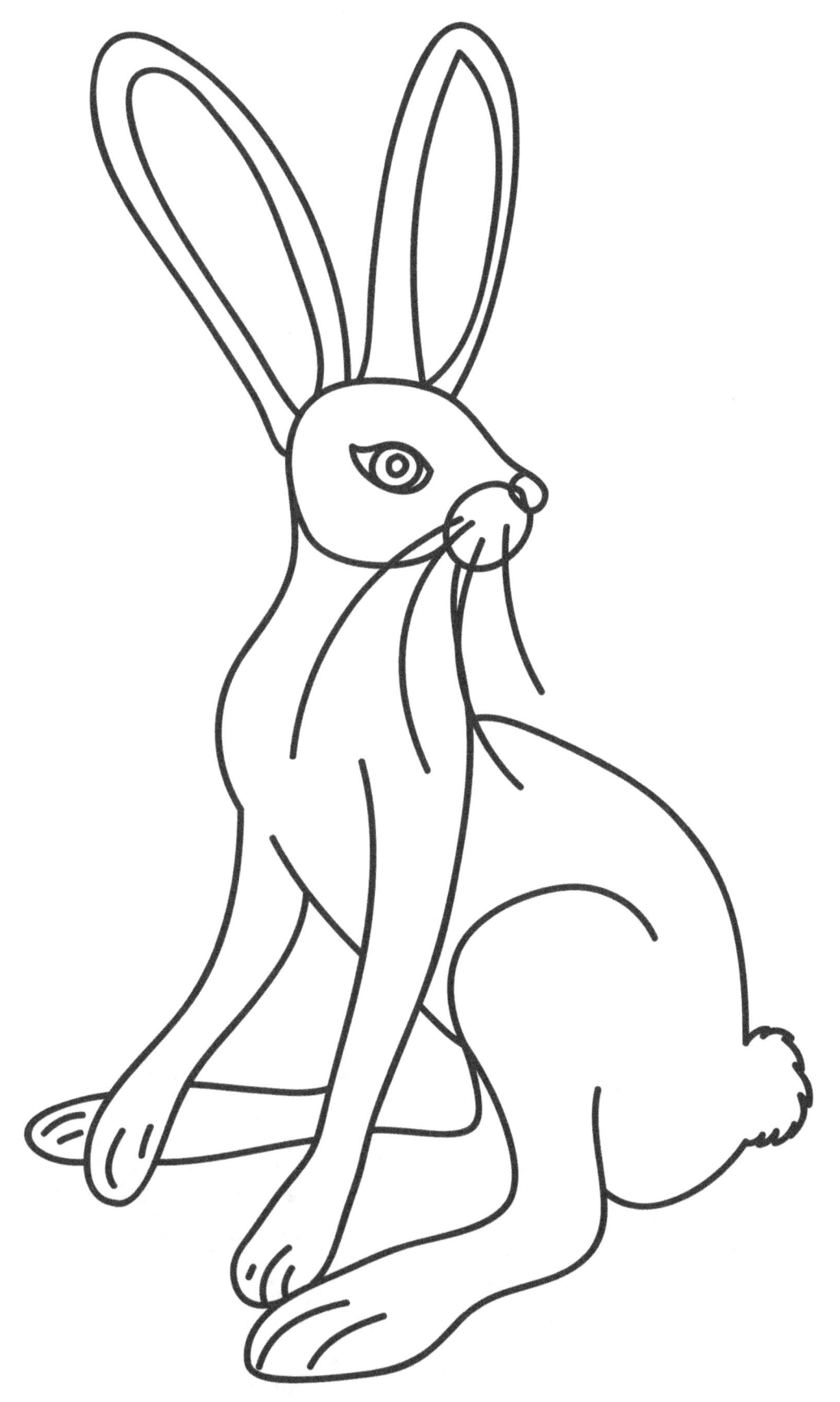

# COLOR TEST PAGE

# COLOR TEST PAGE

www.ingramcontent.com/pod-product-compliance
Lightning Source LLC
Chambersburg PA
CBHW081537220526
45467CB00010B/3224